EXPLORING

THE

GIFTS

OF THE

SPIRIT

ALSO BY JOHN MICHAEL TALBOT
AND STEVE RABEY

*The Lessons of St. Francis: How to Bring Simplicity
and Spirituality into Your Daily Life*
*The Way of the Mystics: Ancient Wisdom
for Experiencing God Today*
The Music of Creation: Foundations of a Christian Life

EXPLORING

THE

GIFTS

OF THE

SPIRIT

DISCOVERING THE POWER

GOD HAS FOR YOU

JOHN MICHAEL TALBOT

WITH STEVE RABEY

EMANATE

BOOKS

Published in Nashville, Tennessee, by Emanate Books, an imprint of Thomas Nelson. Emanate Books and Thomas Nelson are registered trademarks of HarperCollins Christian Publishing, Inc.

Thomas Nelson titles may be purchased in bulk for educational, business, fund-raising, or sales promotional use. For information, please e-mail SpecialMarkets@ThomasNelson.com.

Unless otherwise noted, Scripture quotations are taken from the Holy Bible, New International Version®, NIV®. Copyright © 1973, 1978, 1984, 2011 by Biblica, Inc.® Used by permission of Zondervan. All rights reserved worldwide. www.Zondervan. com. The "NIV" and "New International Version" are trademarks registered in the United States Patent and Trademark Office by Biblica, Inc.®

Scripture quotations marked ESV are from the ESV® Bible (The Holy Bible, English Standard Version®). Copyright © 2001 by Crossway, a publishing ministry of Good News Publishers. Used by permission. All rights reserved.

Scripture quotations marked THE MESSAGE are from *The Message*. Copyright © by Eugene H. Peterson 1993, 1994, 1995, 1996, 2000, 2001, 2002. Used by permission of NavPress. All rights reserved. Represented by Tyndale House Publishers, Inc.

Scripture quotations marked NRSV-CE are from the Catholic Edition of the New Revised Standard Version of the Bible. Copyright 1989, 1993 National Council of the Churches of Christ in the United States of America. Used by permission. All rights reserved.

All song lyrics written by John Michael Talbot, copyright Troubadour for the Lord or Birdwing Music. All rights reserved.

ISBN 978-0-7852-3305-3 (eBook)
ISBN 978-0-7852-3304-6 (TP)

Library of Congress Control Number: 2020931430

Printed in the United States of America
20 21 22 23 24 LSC 10 9 8 7 6 5 4 3 2 1

CONTENTS

PART 3: CONCLUSION

PART I

INTRODUCTION

CHAPTER 1

ALIVE IN GOD'S SPIRIT

All of them were filled with the Holy Spirit.
—ACTS 2:4

It was a confusing time for the disciples. Jesus' violent crucifixion had left many of them fearful and heartbroken. After he rose from the dead, he appeared to some of them, encouraging them, and teaching them over the course of more than a month.

Then, suddenly, he was gone again, ascending gloriously into heaven. He promised his followers that the Holy Spirit would guide them, but they didn't have a clue what that meant.

They found out on the day of Pentecost, when they wound up in the middle of a divine commotion.

Suddenly a sound like the blowing of a violent wind came from heaven and filled the whole house where they were sitting. They saw what seemed to be tongues of fire that separated and came to rest on each of them. All of them were filled with the Holy

Spirit and began to speak in other tongues as the Spirit enabled them. (Acts 2:2–4)

Speaking in tongues was only one of many gifts the Holy Spirit poured out on the men and women who followed Jesus. The Spirit empowered these disciples to make crucial decisions, prophesy about future events, heal the sick, discern the presence of evil spirits, and spread his message throughout the world.

These events were supernatural in origin, not a result of over-excited crowds, and the Spirit's gifts also provided evidence that the fledgling Christian movement was more than merely another new Middle Eastern religious movement. The Christians' God had real, supernatural power on their side.

St. Basil the Great, a fourth-century church father, described the Spirit's role in his classic work *On the Holy Spirit*:

> Just as a sunbeam, falling on light and transparent bodies, makes them exceedingly bright and causes them to pour forth a brilliance from themselves, so too souls which bear the Spirit and which are illuminated by the Spirit become spiritual themselves and send forth grace to others. Hence comes to us foreknowledge of the future, understanding of mysteries, discernment of what is hidden, sharing of good gifts, heavenly citizenship, a place in the choir of angels, joy without cease, abiding in God, likeness unto God, and that which is best of all, being made God.[1]

THE FIRE COOLS

Apparently not everyone shared Basil's positive appraisal of the Spirit's ongoing work in the church. St. John Chrysostom, the

Archbishop of Constantinople, lived during the same time as Basil, but his report was less positive. He complained that the Spirit's work wasn't as powerful as it had been in the good old days.

> The present church is like a woman who has fallen from her former prosperous days. In many respects she retains only the symbols of that ancient prosperity. She displays, in fact, the repositories and the caskets of her gold ornaments, but she is, in fact, deprived of wealth. The present church represents such a woman . . . only the tokens of the charisms remain of those ancient times.[2]

St. Augustine, one of the leading Christian theologians of all time, acknowledged that while he and his fellow theologians had spent much time developing a rich theology about Jesus Christ (known as Christology), they had devoted little attention to the theology of the Holy Spirit (known as Pneumatology). As he wrote in *Faith and the Creed*:

> The subject of the Holy Spirit, however, has not yet been sufficiently nor so diligently treated by the great and learned commentators on the Sacred Scriptures, that we can easily understand what is proper to Him.[3]

Over the centuries, some church leaders quit depending on the Holy Spirit to guide and grow the church, turning instead to administrative abilities, or government power, or marketing techniques. It is as if we tried to dress up the Spirit in an attractive suit and tie to match our cultural preferences. But the Spirit resists such efforts.

Sociologists say such "drift" is typical of how organizations—religious and secular—lose sight of their founding vision over time. Organizations go through life cycles, and that's why they need reformers or "turnaround" CEOs.

The fire of the Spirit that fell at Pentecost has never been extinguished, but has cooled at times over the ages. Today, many people in Catholic, Protestant, evangelical, and Orthodox churches have been baptized in the name of the Father, the Son, and the Holy Spirit. But the active and powerful presence of the Spirit is often missing from their daily Christian experience.

I remember talking to a man who represented this problem. He was a godly man in his forties who worked as a security guard at one of my concerts. He asked me, "What is the Holy Spirit, really?" He was a good Catholic and a leader in his parish. He understood God the Father and Jesus the Son, but he just couldn't understand the Holy Spirit.

He's not alone.

I appreciated his honesty and said that trying to explain God's Spirit is like trying to describe chocolate cake to someone who has never tasted its sweetness. "You will never truly understand this thing called chocolate cake without taking a bite and experiencing it for yourself," I told him as I encouraged him to seek the Spirit's guidance.

RENEWAL AND REVIVAL

The 1960s were a confusing time for people across America. The decade ushered in complex cultural battles over war and peace, love and sex, religion and spirituality, the generation gap, music, and drugs. It was a time when many feared the world would come to an end, either through the destructive power of atomic war or the return of Christ.

By the early 1970s, I was an on-fire, born-again, guitar-playing member of the Jesus movement that had recently swept the nation, drawing many young people to Christ. Thanks to this Jesus movement, I had come back to faith in Jesus after a successful life in rock 'n' roll. I transitioned from a career playing secular country rock to a music ministry focused on what we simply called "Jesus music." This was before it grew into the Contemporary Christian Music—or CCM—industry that continues today.

At the same time, a parallel charismatic movement brought the fire of the Spirit to Catholic, Episcopal, Lutheran, and evangelical churches.

Many of us who came to Christ during these tumultuous times experienced manifestations of God's presence during our conversion experiences, so it was "natural" for us to expect these "supernatural" experiences to continue as we grew in the faith. We spent many hours studying, discussing, and seeking God's spiritual gifts.

When I met Catholic charismatics at my concerts, I saw that they were a sweet people. They seemed to have a gentler spirit than the classical Pentecostals I had met, who traced their history back to the Azusa Street Revival of the early 1900s. Many of the Catholic charismatics I met seemed to have "deep roots." They connected the dots between *their own experience* of the Spirit and *the Spirit's earlier work* throughout church history, including saints, miracles, and mystical theology.

I wanted to know more about the Spirit, but when I searched for greater depth than was offered by the superficial charismatic theology of the day, I found Augustine was right: Pneumatology was a neglected area of contemporary study.

That's when I found myself being drawn to saints and church fathers and the study of church history. Many saints, including St. Francis, embraced the Spirit's power and gifts in their ministry.

As I studied the writings of the church fathers—leaders and scholars who lived during the first few centuries of the church—I saw that they ministered in the power of the Holy Spirit and displayed an evangelical zeal and love for Jesus.

The more I studied church history, I saw a pattern emerge. During times when the fire of the Spirit cooled, God turned the temperature up with movements of renewal and reform. Through my involvement in the charismatic movement, I was participating in the latest of these regular spiritual revivals that God brings from time to time.

Realizing I needed to put my spiritual passion into practice, I moved into a Franciscan retreat center in Indianapolis, where I was immersed in a regional Catholic charismatic movement that was renewing churches there.

In time, I moved out of the retreat center and embraced the life of a hermit. After a few years, a new community of charismatic Catholics began to grow up around me. Out of this shared experience was born the Brothers and Sisters of Charity—a charismatic and contemplative community that remains together decades later.

EMPOWERED BY THE SPIRIT

The apostles lived with Jesus for nearly four years. They heard him teach countless lessons. They saw him work countless miracles, including raising at least three people from the dead. They saw him crucified for his ministry, then, beyond all belief, they saw him raised from the dead!

After all this time, you would think they should have received sufficient guidance and inspiration to prepare them to live according to their master's teaching. But Jesus told them that they didn't yet have everything they would need to fulfill their mission and build his church. He told them to wait in Jerusalem until they were empowered by the Holy Spirit. That promised empowerment was what happened on the day of Pentecost.

I wonder if Christians today face a predicament that's similar to the one Jesus' disciples faced. Many of us attend big churches, hear sermons from highly trained ministers, sing worship songs led by accomplished musicians, and receive the sacraments. We might even consume Christian books, music, or other media.

But have we done what the apostles were commanded to do? Have we been empowered by the Holy Spirit?

In traditional churches, we often mumble through liturgical responses or sing hymns as though we were sleepwalking, enduring such rituals while we wait for a good sermon or a sacramental experience. That's regrettable.

The Spirit can breathe new life and enthusiasm into our liturgical worship, but we must ask for and receive this gift.

Our worship should stir up the Spirit, not stifle it. We should enjoy our times of corporate celebration, not merely endure them. We should be engaged, not bored or daydreaming about lunch.

In contemporary churches, we may sing, dance, or clap along with energetic worship music, some of it written by charismatic worship leaders. But do we realize there's more to worshipping God than hopping up and down and whooping at the top of our lungs in response to a loud, energetic worship band? Has our worship been empowered by the Holy Spirit, or are we merely being entertained and energized by good bands, powerful sound systems, and pulsing lights? Is this spiritual worship or human emotionalism?

On the other hand, many believers around the world today *do* experience the Spirit on a regular basis. I have noticed a deeper interest in the work of the Holy Spirit among members of our community and people I meet at my concerts. I hear reports about the power of the Spirit falling upon people in new and fresh ways through conferences, groups, or movements.

I'm grateful for these signs of life, and I'm hopeful.

At the same time, it seems Christ's church is also suffering. Sexual scandals are rocking not only the Catholic Church but also the Southern Baptists, as well as other groups. The overall percentage of the global population attending church continues to decline. Many congregations are divided between warring groups of "liberals" and "conservatives." The fastest-growing religious group in America is currently the "nones," who embrace no particular religious affiliation.

HOPE IN GOD

In this time of discouragement for many, I want to bring a message of faith and encouragement. I believe that if we petition God to give us the power of his Spirit, he will do so, and is doing so even this moment.

I join with the psalmist in singing:

> Why, my soul, are you downcast?
> Why so disturbed within me?
> Put your hope in God,
> for I will yet praise him,
> my Savior and my God. (Psalm 42:5)

As founder and general minister of a monastic community that integrates the charismatic and the contemplative, the spontaneous and the liturgical, I have enjoyed frequent opportunities to teach on the Holy Spirit.

I have prepared for these opportunities by studying the Spirit's work—from the time of the creation of the cosmos, to the ministries of Christ and his early church, to the Spirit-filled desert fathers and mothers, to the spiritual renewals and revivals of history, even up to the present age.

In this book, I want to share this wealth of wisdom with readers from all Christian traditions who hunger for the Spirit but may not know much about church history, saints, or Pneumatology.

I will also share personal stories from my own decades-long journey as a disciple of Jesus and a charismatic Catholic—not because I claim equality with the Saints, but because I believe you may be encouraged by seeing how even a lowly disciple like myself can receive and use the Spirit's glorious gifts.

I pray you find guidance that will help you experience the Holy Spirit in a more powerful way. Let's start by understanding more about the Spirit who gives us good gifts.

CHAPTER 2

THE SPIRIT AND THE GIFTS

Fan into flame the gift of God.
—2 TIMOTHY 1:6

Who exactly is the Holy Spirit? The Bible uses a variety of words to describe the third person of the Holy Trinity:

- FIRE. The Holy Spirit showed up on the day of Pentecost, appearing in the form of "tongues of fire" (Acts 2:3).
- WIND. Jesus compared the unpredictable Spirit to the blowing of the wind. "The wind blows wherever it pleases. You hear its sound, but you cannot tell where it comes from or where it is going. So it is with everyone born of the Spirit" (John 3:8). The Greek word *pneuma* (breath or wind) is used for the Spirit throughout the New Testament.
- POWER. The Greek word the New Testament uses to describe God's miraculous power is *dunamis,* the root word for our word *dynamite.*

These biblical descriptions are helpful, but there's a contemporary comparison that may be even more helpful: electricity. The power of the Spirit is like the electric wires that run through the walls of our houses. The electricity is there, ready to power our TVs, appliances, and other devices. But for us to access this power, we must *plug in* and *turn on* our devices. Even the most powerful computer won't do you any good unless it has electricity.

The same is true with the power of the Spirit. We must *plug in* and *turn on*. You and I have already received the Spirit through our faith in Christ, baptism, confirmation, the sacraments, the word of God in Scripture, the church, and God's glorious creation. But we must go further to receive the active gift of the Spirit. We must actively engage with the Spirit and seek the Spirit's powerful presence in our lives.

The better we can understand who the Spirit is, and the more we seek to engage this power, the greater our chances of having the Spirit invade and empower our lives.

THE HOLY SPIRIT: A BRIEF HISTORY

Many people seem to believe that the Holy Spirit suddenly appeared for the first time ever on the day of Pentecost, but this overlooks the Spirit's very lengthy history.

THE SPIRIT IN THE OLD TESTAMENT

The Spirit was present with God the Father from the very beginning, "hovering over the waters" at the creation of the cosmos (Genesis 1:2).

It's interesting that the Genesis 1 creation account uses plural "us" language for God rather than a singular "me": "Then God said, 'Let us make mankind in our image, in our likeness'" (Genesis 1:26).

That's because the Spirit is a person—the third person of the Holy Trinity of Father, Son, and Spirit. The Spirit is not an impersonal, disembodied force. This is where my earlier electricity comparison falls short. "Plugging in" to the Spirit is not as simple as putting a power cord in an electrical socket. Rather, it's similar to the process of developing a relationship with another person, except that in this case the other person is God.

More than fifty Old Testament passages explore the work of the Spirit, meaning the Holy Spirit. For example:

- God filled an artisan by the name of Bezalel with his Spirit, empowering Bezalel to perform intricate designs in gold, silver, and bronze for God's tabernacle (Exodus 31:2–4; 35:30–31).
- During Israel's pilgrimage in the desert, God asked Moses to find seventy elders who could help administer the people's needs, giving them some of his Spirit he had placed on Moses (Numbers 11:24–25).
- God also gave his Spirit to Joshua, who would lead Israel to the promised land (Numbers 27:12–23).

Many more passages say God gave "the Spirit of the LORD" to a number of his servants, including little-known figures (Othniel, Jephthah), Old Testament superheroes (Gideon, Samson), and even a donkey (Numbers 22:28). (These are distinct from the nearly 150 Old Testament references to "spirit" with a small *s*, which refers to either the human spirit or false supernatural spirits that are not from God.) The Holy Spirit was certainly present among the Jewish people before the time of Christ, but the Spirit was poured out in a whole new way in a new dispensation beginning at Pentecost.

In one of his psalms, David praised God for the Spirit's presence and accessibility:

> Where can I go from your Spirit?
>> Where can I flee from your presence?
> If I go up to the heavens, you are there;
>> if I make my bed in the depths, you are there.
>
> (Psalm 139:7–8)

THE SPIRIT IN JESUS' MINISTRY

The Holy Spirit was also very active in the life of Jesus, even before Jesus was incarnated and born as a human. The Spirit overshadowed Mary at the conception of Jesus as the incarnation of the Word of God (Luke 1:35). The Spirit was also present in the prophecy of Simeon to Mary, when Jesus was presented at the temple (Luke 2:25).

During Jesus' life on earth, the Holy Spirit was seen in bodily form "like a dove" descending on Jesus at his baptism (Luke 3:22). Then the Spirit led Jesus into the desert to be tempted by the Devil in preparation for his public ministry (Luke 4:1).

Jesus taught extensively about the Holy Spirit and promised his followers they would receive that divine power (John 14:17). Depending on which translation of the New Testament you read, you will see the Spirit described as the comforter, helper, advocate, counselor, intercessor, or friend (John 14:16).

Jesus gave the Holy Spirit to the apostles to empower their leadership before his ascension, but this was merely a foretaste of the spiritual gifts to come (John 20:22).

THE SPIRIT IN THE APOSTOLIC PERIOD

Before his ascension to heaven, Jesus told his disciples about the coming of the Holy Spirit's power.

"Do not leave Jerusalem, but wait for the gift my Father promised, which you have heard me speak about," Jesus told them. "For John baptized with water, but in a few days you will be baptized with the Holy Spirit" (Acts 1:4–5).

Finally, the Holy Spirit descended upon all believers with new power at Pentecost (Acts 2). In the book of Acts, we see the Spirit helping Jesus' followers as they proclaim his gospel and organize the first churches.

As the book of Acts shows, believers who had been baptized in Jesus' name before the Spirit descended were now baptized in the Holy Spirit through the laying on of hands. In one passage, Peter and John travel to Samaria to minister to the Christ followers there.

> When they arrived, they prayed for the new believers there that they might receive the Holy Spirit, because the Holy Spirit had not yet come on any of them; they had simply been baptized in the name of the Lord Jesus. Then Peter and John placed their hands on them, and they received the Holy Spirit. (Acts 8:15–17)

Paul had a similar experience in Ephesus, ministering to believers who had told him, "No, we have not even heard that there is a Holy Spirit" (Acts 19:2).

Throughout the book of Acts, we see the Holy Spirit poured out in a variety of ways on those who accepted Jesus. For example, sometimes the Spirit fell on people through the preaching of the Word of God (Acts 10:4). Sometimes the Spirit fell *before* people were baptized, and sometimes *afterward* (Acts 2:38; 10:47).

Cyril of Jerusalem, the fourth-century theologian who is considered a saint by Catholics, Orthodox believers, and Anglicans/Episcopalians, wrote in his *Catechetical Lectures* about how the same Spirit manifests in a variety of ways:

> One and the same rain comes down on all the world, yet it becomes white in the lily, red in the rose, purple in the violets and hyacinths, different and many-colored in manifold species. Thus it is one in the palm tree and another in the vine, and all in all things, though it is uniform and does not vary in itself. For the rain does not change, coming down now as one thing and now as another, but it adapts itself to the thing receiving it and becomes what is suitable to each. Similarly the Holy Spirit, being One and of one nature and indivisible, imparts to each one his grace "according as he will."[1]

The lesson for us to remember here is that the Spirit cannot be put into a box or controlled by us. As we saw above, "The wind blows wherever it pleases" (John 3:8).

Today, I believe many believers who have already undergone the sacrament of baptism and confirmation need also to receive the baptism of the Spirit to better engage the Spirit's power.

THE GIFTS OF THE HOLY SPIRIT

In his first letter to the Corinthian believers, the apostle Paul described the gifts of the Holy Spirit. As we will see in the chapters to come, the Spirit gives these gifts to believers to empower them for ministry, evangelism, and the building up of Christ's church.

Paul provided different lists of these gifts, and his lists don't always match up. In this book we will explore nine of the Spirit's major gifts described by Paul in 1 Corinthians 12–14:

- Word of wisdom
- Word of knowledge
- Faith
- Healing
- Miracles
- Prophecy
- Discernment of Spirit
- Speaking in tongues
- Interpretation of tongues

THE SPIRIT IN CHURCH HISTORY

More than a century after the Spirit's outpouring on the day of Pentecost, church father Justin Martyr would declare: "There are prophetic gifts among us even until now. You may see with us both women and men having gifts from the Spirit of God."[2]

Justin Martyr declared that the Holy Spirit had prevailed over other spirits that were not from God. As he wrote in *The Second Apology of Justin*:

That the empire of spirits has been destroyed by Jesus you may even now convince yourselves by what is passing before your own eyes; for many of our people, of us Christians, have healed and still continue to heal in every part of the world, and even in your city (Rome) numbers possessed by evil spirits (are healed) such as could not be healed by other exorcists, simply by adjuring them in the name of Jesus Christ, who was crucified under Pontius Pilate.[3]

Irenaeus, bishop of Lyons, France, wrote in *Against Heresies* that the Spirit's gifts were still at work in the mid-to-late second century:

> We also hear many brethren in the Church who possess prophetic gifts, who through the Spirit speak all kinds of languages, and bring to light for the general benefit the hidden things of men and declare the mysteries of God, whom also the apostles term spiritual.[4]

Origen of Alexandria, perhaps the most brilliant thinker during the early centuries of the church, claimed he had personally seen the Spirit's gifts at work in the third century. As he wrote in his treatise *Against Celsus*:

> Some give evidence of having received, through their faith a marvelous power by the cures which they perform, invoking no other Name over those who need their help than that of the God of all things, and of Jesus, along with mention of His history. For by these means we too have seen many persons freed by these means from grievous calamities, and from distractions of mind, and madness, and countless other ills, which could not be cured neither by men or devils.[5]

In his classic book *The City of God*, African bishop Augustine of Hippo (modern-day Algeria) reported on the Spirit's gifts he saw in action in the fourth and fifth centuries. In his eighth chapter, "Of Miracles Which Were Wrought That the World Might Believe in Christ," Augustine included many examples:

For even now miracles are wrought in the name of Christ, whether by His sacraments or by the prayers or relics of His saints. . . . What am I to do? I am so pressed by the promise of finishing this work that I cannot record all the miracles I know. . . .

For were I to be silent of all others, and to record exclusively the miracles of healing which were wrought in the district of Calama and of Hippo by means of this martyr—I mean the most glorious Stephen—they would fill many volumes; and yet all even of these could not be collected, but only those of which narratives have been written for public recital . . . which have been published amount to almost seventy at the hour at which I write. But at Calama, where these relics have been for a longer time, and where more of the miracles were narrated for public information, there are incomparably more.[6]

Part of why I love St. Francis, the thirteenth-century saint, is because he gave birth to a movement that manifested the gifts of the Spirit in powerful and miraculous ways. These spiritual gifts were powerful demonstrations of God's power, and they bore real fruit in transformed lives and strong Christian communities. In addition, Francis helped inspire a medieval peace movement that nearly stopped the feudal wars destroying much of Europe.

I know many Protestants who claim that the Catholic Church is a "dead" institution that relies on rules and procedures, not the Holy Spirit. Many organizations become more institutional over time as they develop from a grassroots movement to a more formal structure.

But these testimonies show that the Spirit's gifts remained active for many centuries, and they are still active today.

ARE THE SPIRIT'S GIFTS
ACTIVE TODAY?

Not everyone is riding on the Spirit train. Not all Christians agree about the Spirit's work. Some denominations promote a "cessationist" theology that claims that most spiritual gifts we read about in the New Testament ceased operating once the church was established and the New Testament was written.

Protestant reformer John Calvin represented this kind of cessationism. "Certainly the gift of tongues and other things of that kind have long since ceased in the Church," he said, "but the Spirit of understanding and regeneration thrives and will always thrive."[7]

Methodist founder John Wesley became more interested in the life of the Spirit during the weeks he sailed from England to America with a group of charismatic Moravian believers, but he never gave himself over to a life of signs and wonders. He remained cautious about the more overtly miraculous manifestations of the Spirit, even after he experienced such manifestations himself personally. This remained a theological tension for Wesley throughout his life. The Methodist movement he founded spoke of a "Second Blessing" as a kind of deeper sanctification through the Holy Spirit, and helped pave the way for later movements of spiritual renewal.

There are many today who teach that the gifts of the Spirit ceased operating after the first century. These believers don't know what to do with people like me who have witnessed these gifts at work in the twenty-first century. They dismiss us as nutcases, heretics, or even demoniacs.

The criticism doesn't really hurt me. What does worry me is that believers who are convinced the Spirit's gifts stopped long ago are closing themselves off from receiving gifts the Spirit wishes to give them.

Wonderful things can happen in the church if we will but open ourselves to the real power of the Holy Spirit, and that's why I appreciate the approach St. Augustine took. Early in his Christian life, St. Augustine was a cessationist who believed the Spirit's gifts ceased after the early church was established. But after he became bishop of Hippo and clearly saw that the Spirit's gifts were fully functioning in his local church, he changed his tune.

I believe we should continually ask God to bless his people with his Spirit. As David wrote in his beautiful Psalm 104, God's Spirit revises and empowers all his creatures on earth:

> When you send your Spirit,
>> they are created,
>> and you renew the face of the ground. (v. 30)

I adapted the words of David's psalm to create my own song, "Lord, Send Forth Your Spirit." Singing this song, as we do at our annual Easter Vigil at Little Portion Hermitage, helps me pray to God for the Spirit's power:

> Lord, send forth your Spirit and renew the face of the Earth.
> Lord, send forth your Spirit and renew the face of the Earth.
> Bless the Lord O my soul you are great indeed;
> Clothed with light and majesty, robed with light and glory.
> You fixed the earth on foundations, never more to be moved.
> As with the cloak you covered her, above the waters stood.
> You send forth streams and rivers
> that wind among the mountains and the hills

Beside them the birds of heaven dwell
from their branches send forth their singing.
You water the earth from your palace
the earth is replete with your works
raising grass and vegetation, producing bread from the earth.
Lord, send forth your Spirit, create all of the world.
Lord, send forth your Spirit, create all the world, all the world.

INDWELT, FILLED, AND SEALED?

I occasionally wish there was a detailed operating manual for the Holy Spirit that would help me better understand how all this works. Paul wrote extensively about the work of the Spirit, but he often sounded like he was struggling to explain it all. He even admitted there was much he didn't know:

> For now we see only a reflection as in a mirror; then we shall see face to face. Now I know in part; then I shall know fully, even as I am fully known. (1 Corinthians 13:12)

Our knowledge about all three of the persons of God is limited, but most believers feel they understand the Father and the Son better than the Spirit, who remains somewhat mysterious.

The New Testament uses various words to describe the Spirit's presence in our lives, including three that are often confused: *indwelt*, *filled*, and *sealed*. Let me help make sense of these terms, based on my study and personal experience.

We are indwelt by the Spirit (Romans 8:9). Being *indwelt* by the Spirit means having his constant and gentle divine presence in our lives, despite the ups and downs of daily existence. Catholic theology calls this *habitual grace*.

We are also filled with the Spirit (Acts 2:2; Ephesians 5:18). Being *filled* is what happens when we are on fire for God in Christ and living lives of holiness. This is called *actual grace*.

Being *sealed* by the Spirit is part of the process of conversion to Jesus that protects us from outside corruption. This is seen in the *sacramental grace* of confirmation of chrismation.

THEOLOGY OF THE HOLY SPIRIT

A brief review of the basics of Pneumatology can help us have a better understanding of the Spirit who gives us such wonderful gifts.

First and foremost, experiencing the Holy Spirit should be part of life for every Christian, not just an elite super-spiritual few.

- Jesus taught that we must be born from above by the Holy Spirit (John 3:3).
- He promised that the Spirit would supernaturally guide us unto all truth, and that through the Spirit he himself remains present with us (John 16:13).
- Peter preached to the crowd on the day of Pentecost: "Repent and be baptized, every one of you, in the name of Jesus Christ for the forgiveness of your sins. And you will receive the gift of the Holy Spirit" (Acts 2:38).
- Paul said that we cannot even call Jesus "Lord" unless we do so by the Spirit (1 Corinthians 12:3).
- And as Paul told us, "Do not grieve the Holy Spirit of God, with whom you were sealed for the day of redemption" (Ephesians 4:30).

SPIRIT VS. FLESH

You and I have a choice. We can plug into God's divine power, or we can try to do things on our own. The results couldn't be more different. This powerful passage from Paul shows the difference between living in the Spirit and living the life of the flesh:

> For those who live according to the flesh set their minds on the things of the flesh, but those who live according to the Spirit set their minds on the things of the Spirit. For to set the mind on the flesh is death, but to set the mind on the Spirit is life and peace. For the mind that is set on the flesh is hostile to God, for it does not submit to God's law; indeed, it cannot. Those who are in the flesh cannot please God.
>
> You, however, are not in the flesh but in the Spirit, if in fact the Spirit of God dwells in you. Anyone who does not have the Spirit of Christ does not belong to him. But if Christ is in you, although the body is dead because of sin, the Spirit is life because of righteousness. If the Spirit of him who raised Jesus from the dead dwells in you, he who raised Christ Jesus from the dead will also give life to your mortal bodies through his Spirit who dwells in you. (Romans 8:5–11 ESV)

When the Spirit appeared at Pentecost, observers believed the Christians were drunk on wine, but Paul made an important distinction between alcoholic spirits and God's Holy Spirit, writing to the Ephesian Christians: "Do not get drunk on wine, which leads to debauchery. Instead, be filled with the Spirit" (Ephesians 5:18).

Most of us have probably received the Holy Spirit through baptism, confirmation, the Eucharist, prayer, and devotion. As St. Athanasius argued in his *Discourses Against the Arians*:

It is, then, through the grace given us of the Spirit, that we come to be in Him, and He in us; and since this Spirit is the Spirit of God, through His coming to be in us and our having the Spirit, we are reasonably considered as coming to be in God; and thus, God is in us.[8]

We are *indwelled* by the Spirit, but have we experienced the dynamic empowerment of being *filled* by the Holy Spirit? Have we plugged in to the Spirit's powerful gifts?

"FAN INTO FLAME THE GIFT OF GOD"

"Fan into flame the gift of God." That was Paul's message to Timothy (2 Timothy 1:6). He was probably referring to both Timothy's gift of ordained ministry and leadership and, more broadly, the power of the Holy Spirit in our lives.

That's my message to you in this book: "Fan into flame the gift of God."

Fanning the Spirit's gifts into flame may be similar to stirring up a big glass of chocolate milk. Those of you who are fans of this delicious beverage will know what I'm talking about. You pour the milk into the glass and then add the chocolate syrup. But before you know it the chocolate settles to the bottom of the glass. Yes, it is down there somewhere, but it keeps to itself and doesn't permeate the milk. The milk still pretty much looks and tastes as it did before.

One thing is lacking: the chocolate must be stirred up before it permeates the milk and changes its substance.

The same thing is true with the Holy Spirit. He is present in all Christians. He indwells us. Perhaps the Spirit that is present in your life must be stirred up. You need to "plug in" before this power fills and permeates your entire life.

How do we do this? You and I must activate the Spirit's presence that is already within us. And we must humbly seek the additional gifts the Holy Spirit lavishes upon Christ's followers. We do this by actively asking for these gifts, and responding to what we are given.

My spiritual father taught me this with a simple illustration. He handed a book to me, but asked me not to reach out to receive it. The book stayed in his hand. Then, he handed the book to me again, but asked me to respond by reaching to receive it. Now the book was in my hands. The lesson was clear. Gifts might be offered, but unless we reach out to receive them, we will never receive these gifts.

We stir up the Spirit through our thanksgiving and praise (Psalm 100; Ephesians 5:20). With the gift of tongues, we should ask for this gift, then dare to open our mouths and make some noise! If we say we want the gifts but fail to take appropriate action to receive and stir them up, we will never experience them in our lives.

I wrote a song called "Fan into Flame" that expands on Paul's message to Timothy. The song can serve as a kind of prayer as we seek God's Spirit in our lives:

I remind you now to fan into flame
The gift that God has bestowed
When my hands were laid upon you,
The gift of the Spirit of God.
The gift that God has given to us,
Is no cowardly spirit at all.
But one that is strong and loving and wise—

The gift of the Spirit of God.
So you, my son, you must be strong,
In the grace which is yours in Christ.
The teaching you have heard through me,
Hand onto the trustworthy ones.
The Spirit, God has given to us
Is no cowardly spirit at all.
But one that is strong and loving and wise—
The gift of the Spirit of God,
The gift of the Spirit of God.

The Holy Spirit is alive and well in the twenty-first century. Are we plugging in to that power?

One way to experience the Spirit is through the Spirit's gifts. Each gift is unique. Let's explore the nine major gifts Paul described to see how they work and what miracles they can bring.

PART 2

THE GIFTS

CHAPTER 3

THE GIFTS OF TONGUES AND INTERPRETATION

SPEAKING THE LANGUAGES OF MORTALS AND ANGELS

All of them were filled with the Holy Spirit and began
to speak in other tongues as the Spirit enabled them.
—ACTS 2:4

Jews from around the Middle East had gathered in Jerusalem for the annual Jewish holiday of Pentecost. But *this* Pentecost would be something different, as we see in the book of Acts:

When the day of Pentecost came, they were all together in one place. Suddenly a sound like the blowing of a violent wind came from heaven and filled the whole house where they were sitting. They saw what seemed to be tongues of fire that separated and came to rest on each of them. All of them were filled with the Holy Spirit and began to speak in other tongues as the Spirit enabled them.

Now there were staying in Jerusalem God-fearing Jews from every nation under heaven. When they heard this sound, a crowd came together in bewilderment, because each one heard their own language being spoken. Utterly amazed, they asked: "Aren't all these who are speaking Galileans? Then how is it that each of us hears them in our native language? Parthians, Medes and Elamites; residents of Mesopotamia, Judea and Cappadocia, Pontus and Asia, Phrygia and Pamphylia, Egypt and the parts of Libya near Cyrene; visitors from Rome (both Jews and converts to Judaism); Cretans and Arabs—we hear them declaring the wonders of God in our own tongues!"

Amazed and perplexed, they asked one another, "What does this mean?" Some, however, made fun of them and said, "They have had too much wine." (Acts 2:1–13)

Finally, Peter stood up with the other eleven apostles and explained the outburst to the confused crowd.

"These people are not drunk, as you suppose. It's only nine in the morning! No, this is what was spoken by the prophet Joel: 'In the last days, God says, I will pour out my Spirit on all people. . . . And everyone who calls on the name of the Lord will be saved.'" (vv. 15–17, 21)

AN UNPREDICTABLE GIFT

Ever since that wild and historic Pentecost day, God's gift of tongues has continued to play an important role in God's universal church. In my life as a Catholic charismatic, I have experienced tongues in these three ways:

1. PROCLAIMING THE GOSPEL TO THOSE WHO HAVEN'T HEARD IT: Helping evangelists reach those who don't speak their language, as we saw in the second chapter of Acts.
2. PROCLAIMING TO THE ASSEMBLY: Speaking in a tongue during corporate worship, which requires interpretation in order for it to be understood and build up the body.
3. PRAYING IN THE SPIRIT: Private prayer in tongues that builds up the person praying either in private or in corporate worship. Paul urged believers to "pray in the Spirit on all occasions with all kinds of prayers and requests" (Ephesians 6:18).

It was this third manifestation—the role of tongues as a private prayer language—that served as my introduction to this unique spiritual gift, as it has for many charismatics.

I never tried to seek out the gift of tongues, but the gift *sought me out* during one of my regular commutes by plane from my farm in Indiana to Los Angeles, then home to my recording studio, Sparrow Records.

I was sitting in my window seat on a flight to LA. It was a brilliant, beautiful, clear day, and as I looked at the clouds, I silently praised God for their wonder and beauty. The next thing I knew, I was praying audibly in a language that wasn't English.

It was a morning flight, so nobody accused me of being drunk, but the frequent-flyer businessman sitting across the aisle gave me a quizzical look I can still remember to this day!

DAILY DISCIPLINES

Tongues seemed to be a spiritual doorway that I had to go through to experience more of the Holy Spirit's presence in my life. Because speaking in tongues provides a similar doorway for many believers, and because tongues generate controversy among some, we will explore this gift first, and then incorporate the gift of interpretation of tongues.

Praying in tongues has become a vital and regular part of my daily prayer times with God. As a Spirit-filled founder of a monastic community, my prayer life is a balance of contemplative and charismatic practices. I also incorporate monastic and liturgical spiritual disciplines that Christians have followed for centuries.

For example, I pray the Liturgy of the Hours, which consists of the Psalms and scripture readings, and ancient prayers designed to sanctify each hour of the day. I prayerfully participate in the Catholic Mass, and pray other devotions like the Jesus Prayer and the Rosary.

Monks love encountering Christ in silence and solitude, also known as contemplation. Jesuit priest Fr. Bob Faricy calls tongues "noisy contemplation," a description that captures this combination well.

During some periods of prayer, I find my brain getting bogged down in all the mental concepts of religion, or even my own sinful thoughts. At these "stuck" times, the Spirit's gift of tongues gets me unstuck, bringing a divine power and warmth that energizes my prayer life. At times, it seems as though the Spirit takes an S.O.S. soap pad to my brain, cleaning away all the layers of gunk, guiding my prayers upward and outward, and empowering me to praise God as I am released from my old self and born again to God.

Many Christians realize that following Jesus is more than just an idea, mental concept, or system of beliefs. We need to go beyond the purely objective to grow in our love for Jesus. Since the time of Christ, many of his followers have sought a mystical dimension in their relationship with Jesus that goes beyond concepts and words.

But this doesn't mean we do away with objectivity, rationality, God's revelation in Scripture, apostolic tradition, or the teaching of the church. It simply means we realize that rationality isn't everything, either in discipleship or in marriage. Having been with my wife, Viola, for decades, I know her pretty well by now. But if our marriage existed only on the intellectual or conceptual level, it wouldn't be a very deep or loving union.

"God is spirit," said Jesus, "and his worshipers must worship in the Spirit and in truth" (John 4:24). The truth we receive through Scripture and the study of church history and theology help us avoid the worship of false or evil spirits. The Spirit also plants God's truth in our lives and guards that truth with the Spirit's power.

God desires our love, and real love requires us to move beyond mere objective *facts about* God to deep expressions of our *love for* God. Tongues, and the other gifts of the Spirit, can help us know, experience, and love God more deeply than we can on our own.

TONGUES—OFTEN CONTROVERSIAL

Over the centuries, babbling believers have caused controversy, divided churches, and generated accusations of drunkenness, insanity, and even demonic possession. Some of the criticism has been justified.

On the other hand, we see that tongues and other gifts have repeatedly accompanied God-inspired movements of revival, reform, renewal, social outreach, and Christian community.

There were two major outpourings of the Spirit in the twentieth century:

- The Azusa revival of the early 1900s gave birth to a new Pentecostal movement that embraced the present-day practice of spiritual gifts like tongues. The Azusa revival, along with outbreaks of the Spirit in Hot Springs, Arkansas, and Topeka, Kansas, spread rapidly and widely, influencing the Salvation Army and giving birth to some of the historic Pentecostal denominations, such as the Assemblies of God. (During the same time, Blessed Elena Guerra, founder of the Oblate Sisters of the Holy Spirit in Italy, was promoting renewal in the Catholic Church. "Pentecost is not over," she said.)
- In the 1960s, a booming charismatic renewal movement introduced believers across many Christian traditions and denominations to the spiritual gifts.

Over the long haul, the three main Christian traditions—Catholic, Orthodox, and Protestant—haven't always known what to do about the Spirit's gifts, but they've mostly tried to follow the guidance of the apostle Paul, who taught: "Do not forbid speaking in tongues" (1 Corinthians 14:39).

Let's see how this unique gift has worked in the past and find out what role it can play in your life today.

THE SOUND OF SALVATION

When the Spirit gave the gift of tongues on the day of Pentecost, people from different regions heard their distinctive languages being spoken. Church history shows that this manifestation of tongues has continued to the present day.

Mark Rutland was in Mexico with a group of fellow Americans on a short-term missions trip with the Assemblies of God, a Pentecostal denomination, when the unexpected happened. After preaching at small, rural churches with the help of an interpreter, he arrived at another church, but his translator didn't show up.

Rutland didn't know Spanish, so he asked the rural church's pastor to preach in his place. But before the Mexican pastor spoke, Rutland said a brief hello to the seventy people present, using the one or two sentences of Spanish he could speak.

Then, before he knew it, his tongue was loosened and he began speaking to the people using Spanish words and sentences he didn't understand.

"It's the Lord!" said Rutland. "Something's going on! It's a miracle, I think."

Rutland's story is just one of eighty accounts of believers speaking in human languages they didn't understand that are gathered together in the book *Global Witnesses to Pentecost: The Testimony of "Other Tongues."*[1]

I can see St. Peter cheering on those who've likewise been gifted with tongues so they can communicate the gospel to those who need to hear it. Such cases have been reported throughout the past twenty centuries of Christian history.

St. Francis Xavier, the Jesuit missionary who preached the gospel throughout Asia during the sixteenth century, reportedly preached in languages he did not know. And St. Vincent Ferrer found that when he preached in his own language people who spoke other languages could understand him.

In the thirteenth century, St. Anthony of Padua, Portugal, became a follower of St. Francis and a friar in the Franciscan movement. Friars were expected to teach and preach, and as we read in *The Little Flowers of St. Francis*, Anthony experienced divine assistance during some of his sermons:

> Being inflamed by the Holy Spirit and inspired with apostolic eloquence, he preached and explained the word of God so effectively, devoutly, subtly, clearly and understandably that all who were assembled at that Consistory, although they spoke different languages, clearly and distinctly heard and understood every one of his words as if he had spoken in each of their languages. Therefore they were all astounded and filled with devotion, for it seemed to them that the former miracle of the Apostles at the time of Pentecost had been renewed, when by the power of the Holy Spirit they spoke in different languages.[2]

Today, one hears numerous stories of Christian missionaries who minister to Muslims suddenly speaking Arabic. In many cases, Muslims reported seeing Jesus in dreams or visions, but they didn't realize who he was until a Christian told them about the gospel.

Only God knows why the Holy Spirit chooses to bless some people with the ability to speak in languages they don't know, but if you are interested in missionary work, I wouldn't rely on this kind of miraculous intervention on a daily basis. God gives his gifts whenever he wills, but meanwhile, missionaries seeking to share the gospel in foreign lands should not abandon their foreign languages lessons, Scripture translations, and cultural and religious studies.

A SIGN OF SALVATION

In the early years of the Christian movement, the gift of tongues frequently served as an exterior sign of interior salvation, as we see throughout the book of Acts.

On the day of Pentecost, tongues helped believers preach the gospel to Jews in their own languages. But once Christians began evangelizing non-Jewish Gentiles, tongues showed that Gentile conversions were authentic:

> The circumcised believers who had come with Peter were astonished that the gift of the Holy Spirit had been poured out even on Gentiles. For they heard them speaking in tongues and praising God.
>
> Then Peter said, "Surely no one can stand in the way of their being baptized with water. They have received the Holy Spirit just as we have." (Acts 10:45–47)

In another case, Paul visited believers in Ephesus and asked them, "Did you receive the Holy Spirit when you believed?" Paul's question puzzled the Ephesian Christians.

"No, we have not even heard that there is a Holy Spirit."

Following a brief discussion about baptism, Paul placed his hands on them. "The Holy Spirit came on them, and they spoke in tongues and prophesied. There were about twelve men in all" (Acts 19:1–7).

Today, pastors and evangelists around the world report that outbursts of tongues accompany conversion and growth in the Spirit.

CORPORATE WORSHIP: TONGUES AND INTERPRETATION IN HARMONY

The early church grew rapidly following the day of Pentecost, and it should come as no surprise that speaking in tongues was a regular feature of corporate worship. So, the Spirit also gave the church a companion gift that would help everyone appreciate the messages spoken in tongues: interpretation.

Paul included both gifts—tongues and interpretation—in this famous passage:

> Now to each one the manifestation of the Spirit is given for the common good. To one there is given through the Spirit a message of wisdom, to another a message of knowledge by means of the same Spirit, to another faith by the same Spirit, to another gifts of healing by that one Spirit, to another miraculous powers, to another prophecy, to another distinguishing between spirits, to another speaking in different kinds of tongues, and to still another the interpretation of tongues. All these are the work of one and the same Spirit, and he distributes them to each one, just as he determines. (1 Corinthians 12:7–11)

Paul made it clear that the gift of tongues is given "for the common good," and interpretation makes this a reality in communal worship, allowing everyone present to hear the message originally expressed in tongues.

Now, brothers and sisters, if I come to you and speak in tongues, what good will I be to you, unless I bring you some revelation or knowledge or prophecy or word of instruction? . . . So it is with you. Unless you speak intelligible words with your tongue, how will anyone know what you are saying? You will just be speaking into the air. . . . Since you are eager for gifts of the Spirit, try to excel in those that build up the church. For this reason the one who speaks in a tongue should pray that they may interpret what they say. (1 Corinthians 14:6, 9, 12–13)

St. John Chrysostom was a pastor and important church father during the fourth century. He disagreed with those who claimed the gift of tongues was useless, but he stressed Paul's teaching that, in church, tongues should only be used for the "common good."

"If speaking in tongues is useless, why was it given?" Chrysostom asked in his commentary on 1 Corinthians. "It was given for the benefit of the person who has it. But if it is to help others also, then there must be some interpretation."[3]

TONGUES MAY HELP *YOU*, BUT INTERPRETATION HELPS *US*

The first time I experienced the paired gifts of tongues and interpretation was during a prayer meeting at Marian University in Indianapolis. As we were praying, an older gentleman stood up and began speaking in tongues in a loud voice. He was dead serious about what he was saying, but it all sounded like gibberish to me.

He sat down. We all fell silent and waited. It wasn't long before someone spoke an interpretation that sounded both challenging and encouraging. In other cases, I have heard the same person speak in an unknown tongue *and* give the interpretation.

I have been privileged to receive the gift of interpretation when needed in our Little Portion community, but I must confess, it took me a long while to become a good and faithful steward of this gift. I use it rarely and with discernment.

There are times during our community worship services when a brother or sister will speak out, addressing the entire assembly in tongues. In the early years of our community, I was hesitant to provide an interpretation, even when God gave me one. I was either too timid to speak up or did not want to be overbearing.

Faced with my resistance and silence, God simply turned to another person in the community to give the interpretation, which would be similar to the interpretation I had received. At the time, I concluded that God's word would go forth, and that if I wouldn't cooperate, someone else would.

A few times I have been in gatherings where a tongue was proclaimed, but there was no interpretation given. Such occasions may indicate that:

- there's someone like me in the group who has received an interpretation but is keeping his mouth shut;
- or this tongue-speaking was not of the Spirit, or not for the common good.

ORDER IN GOD'S HOUSE

Christianity is not the only faith whose adherents speak in tongues. The practice is common among pagan and shamanistic religions, and among mediums practicing spiritism or speaking with the dead. The Dalai Lama has said he consults a shaman who speaks in tongues, and disciples of Krishna Consciousness have reportedly spoken and sung in tongues.

It shouldn't surprise us that God's gifts to his church appear in other guises in other faiths. This simply shows there is a deep human need to transcend rationality to a mystical experience beyond thought or mind, and it makes it even more important that we follow John's advice to be wise and discerning: "Dear friends, do not believe every spirit, but test the spirits to see whether they are from God, because many false prophets have gone out into the world" (1 John 4:1; see chapter 10 of this book).

When God's spiritual gifts came to the Corinthian Christians, the city had already been a center of pagan spirituality for centuries. Corinth was home to ancient pagan temples devoted to Apollo and Athena, Roman temples to Aphrodite, and more. It's no wonder the Corinthian church went wild when the Holy Spirit's gift of tongues arrived.

Paul gave these spiritually confused Corinthians four basic principles governing the practice of tongues during worship services:

1. "Now to each one the manifestation of the Spirit is given for the common good" (1 Corinthians 12:7).

    The point here is that God gives different gifts to different people for "the common good." Paul says tongues aren't for everybody.

2. "If anyone speaks in a tongue, two—or at the most three— should speak, one at a time, and someone must interpret" (1 Corinthians 14:27).

    Here, Paul addresses tongues that are proclaimed to the assembly, making it clear that tongues may play a role in worship, but they aren't to dominate. And if other believers are to benefit from the tongues that are spoken, someone should interpret the message.

3. "I thank God that I speak in tongues more than all of you. But in the church I would rather speak five intelligible words to instruct others than ten thousand words in a tongue" (1 Corinthians 14:18–19).

   Tongues can be helpful, but using language people understand to clearly teach God's truth is far more important than going gaga about this one particular gift.

4. "If I speak in the tongues of men or of angels, but do not have love, I am only a resounding gong or a clanging cymbal" (1 Corinthians 13:1).

   Ultimately, it's all about love. Using God's gifts can be truly powerful when we embody God's heart of love for us all.

Paul's four guidelines govern what happens when we gather together in church, not the use of tongues as foreign languages in evangelism or the use of a private prayer language. The charismatic churches and prayer groups I have been a part of generally follow Paul's guidelines. Gatherings begin with a period of worship and praise during which the gifts of the Spirit might manifest. This is followed by a teaching or a word, a prayer time of petitions and intercessions, and a concluding prayer.

In charismatic Masses, the Spirit's gifts do not overtake or replace the liturgy, but instead enliven and strengthen it. Such Masses typically begin with a few praise and worship songs, allowing singing in the Spirit to be manifested. The ordinary readings, homily, and profession of faith follow. Petitions and intercessions might include spontaneous prayers from the congregation. Additional singing and praying in the Spirit might occur during other portions of the Mass: Preparation of the Gifts; the Sanctus, where we join the choirs of angelic hosts in praise and adoration; or the Epiclesis, where the Spirit is invoked over the elements and the congregation. After Communion, there might be prayers for healing and concluding songs.

It is beautiful to see the Spirit's gifts at work for the common good in corporate worship.

There can be charismatic worship *and* order in God's house if we follow Paul's guidelines. When we do so, the Spirit's gifts function in a beautiful and edifying way. When not, it can get real weird, real fast. I've seen both, and the ordered way is definitely better.

SINGING IN THE SPIRIT

As Paul wrapped up his discussion of the Spirit's gifts, he mentioned another of the Spirit's blessings. "I will sing with my spirit," he wrote (1 Corinthians 14:15).

In my experience, this isn't a separate gift of the Spirit, but more of a musical adaptation of an existing gift. Singing in the Spirit is simply a musical version of speaking in tongues, and this blessing is beneficial, both in private prayer and in corporate worship, where it requires no interpretation.

In past centuries, singing in tongues was often referred to as jubilation. St. Augustine, the brilliant theologian, philosopher, and writer, initially doubted the significance of the spiritual gifts. But after he settled in as bishop of Hippo (in modern-day Algeria), he witnessed too many miracles to continue as a doubter. He described many of the healings he witnessed but could not list them all, for they would have been too many to write down.

Augustine also described singing in the Spirit, which he called jubilation, in his *Exposition of the Psalms*:

> Words cannot express the things that are sung by the heart. . . .
> Such a cry of joy is a sound signifying that the heart is bringing
> to birth what it cannot utter in words. Now who is more worthy
> of such a cry of jubilation than God himself, whom all words
> fail to describe? If words will not serve, and yet you must not
> remain silent, what else can you do but cry out for joy? Your
> heart must rejoice beyond words, that your unbounded joy may
> be unrestrained by syllabic bonds.[4]

One of the beautiful things about singing in the Spirit is that
other people can hear the spiritual quality of the singing, whether
they are devoted disciples or unbelievers. I have worshipped in
many churches, and have heard how the quality of the singing can
vary widely. But when people sing in the Spirit, you can discern
the warmth, lightness, fervency, and heavenly harmony.

My mother accompanied me to a charismatic Mass in
Indianapolis after I had become a Catholic. Though she was a
loyal, hymn-singing member of the United Methodist Church,
she was deeply touched when she heard charismatic Catholics
sweetly and gently singing in the Spirit. She told me later she felt
as though she was hearing the music of heaven. This experience
was one of many that led this once very proper and conservative
woman into a much deeper experience of her faith.

SEEKING AND ACCEPTING GOD'S GIFTS

Even though Paul suggested tongues are a minor gift when compared to interpretation or prophecy, they have played an important
role in the life of believers and the mission of the church throughout history.

What about you? Do you speak in tongues? If not, should you? Whether we are speaking about tongues or the other spiritual gifts we are exploring in this book, these general principles hold true:

- Humbly seek God's good gifts.
- Gratefully accept the gifts the Holy Spirit gives you.
- Strive to be a good steward of the gifts you have received.
- Don't get bent out of shape if God gives good gifts to others instead of you.

Seeking God's gifts is legitimate if you follow these principles. If you want to find out if God has given you the gift of tongues, I recommend you simply try it. Open your mouth and speak some sounds. If we say we want the gift of tongues but refuse to open our mouths, we may never receive it!

Some people say, "Tongues may be great for others, but not for me!" In some cases, this may be a cop-out by people who would be embarrassed to seem silly or out of control. What they're really saying is: "I will do anything for God, except speak in tongues like those irrational, unsophisticated charismatic babblers."

But don't let your pride prevent you from experiencing the unfettered power of the Spirit. I encourage people to seek the gift of tongues before concluding that this particular gift is not for them.

If you are intimidated or embarrassed by doing this in public, go to a private place and try speaking or singing in tongues. Go to the forest, like St. Francis, who out of humility kept his visitations from the Spirit private. But once he was in solitude, he would fill the woods with his loud sighs and groans.

You may want to try singing in the Spirit in your shower! God knows, that's where many people develop the courage to sing!

Even better, participate in a charismatic prayer group or community where you will receive support and guidance in your quest.

I heard a testimony from a Catholic priest about how Pope John Paul II sought the gift of a private tongue for prayer, or a *prayer language*. The pope asked the priest to lay hands on him and pray that he would receive this gift, but apparently the gift did not appear.

The pope kept at it, praying for the gift in private over the next few months. Finally, one day, there was a breakthrough.

"I got the tongues!" the pope shouted out one day. "I got the tongues!"

Be humble. Seek God's gift. Take action to receive the gift. Then accept what happens. If the gift is not given, move on. If the gift is given, follow the advice of Nike: "Just do it!"

SONG FOR A SEEKER

Prayer is one way to invite the Holy Spirit into our hearts. Music can also be a powerful tool to help us as we try to open ourselves to God's will in our lives and receive the gifts he has for us. Music that helps us worship God combines our minds, hearts, spirits, and physical bodies in an expression of love, trust, submission, and openness.

One song of mine that seeks to invite the Spirit into our midst is "Veni Sancte Spiritus," which is Latin for "Come Holy Spirit." Listen to the song, which has a simple melody, and then you can pray this song—or even just the chorus—to God while you are in your prayer time:

Holy Spirit, Lord of Light
From the clear celestial height
Thy pure beaming radiance give
Come, thou father of the poor
Come, with treasures to endure
Come, thou light of all that live
Light immortal, light divine
Visit now, these hearts of thine
And our inmost being fill
For without thy grace, all turns to ill
Veni, Sancte Spiritus . . .
Heal our wounds, our strength renew
On our dryness pour thy dew
Wash the stains of guilt away
Bend our stubborn heart and will
Melt the frozen, warm the chill
Guide our steps when we go astray
Veni, Sancte Spiritus . . .

IT'S GOD'S CALL

God can use any means he chooses to touch us, move us, strengthen us, heal us, and empower us. Tongues is just one of the Spirit's good methods.

Is this gift for you? Only you and God can find out for sure.

CHAPTER 4

THE GIFT OF WISDOM

DIVINE INSIGHTS FOR DAILY LIFE

This is what we speak, not in words taught us by
human wisdom but in words taught by the Spirit.
—1 CORINTHIANS 2:13

Wisdom was there in the very beginning, guiding the creation of the cosmos.

Wisdom revealed the one true God to the Jewish people, and spoke truth through their prophets and teachers.

Wisdom gave herself to King Solomon, a man who sought her with his whole heart and would become world renowned for sharing her with the world.

Wisdom filled Jesus, the Son of God who worked miracles and taught people about the kingdom of heaven through parables.

The Holy Spirit gave a special gift of wisdom to Jesus' disciples. This gift would guide and empower them as they proclaimed his gospel and created the first churches.

The Spirit has been sharing this powerful gift with believers ever since. History shows that at times people have sought and used this gift to serve God and love their neighbors, while at other times we've neglected it, preferring to rely on our own understanding.

And wisdom will be there to the very end, as it is one of the divine characteristics that angels cite as they encircle God's throne and sing his praises:

"Amen! Praise and glory and wisdom and thanks and honor and power and strength be to our God for ever and ever. Amen!" (Revelation 7:12).

Come join me on a brief journey through the history of wisdom, from its ancient roots to today.

HELP NEEDED!

Wisdom has a long and important history, and I believe we need this gift more than ever today, a time when we are drowning in data but starving for wisdom.

We create 2.5 quintillion bytes of data every day, according to an article in the business publication Forbes.com.[1] That's 2,500,000,000,000,000,000 bytes that constantly speed around the world through our texts, emails, tweets, social media posts, photo and video uploads, websites, and more.

Few of us believe this digital data dump represents humanity's best source of wisdom because, as we've seen all too often, some of these sources regularly give us misinformation, falsehoods, "fake news," conspiracy theories, and even abusive hate speech.

People ask me about tongues much more frequently than they ask about wisdom. That's why we explored tongues first.

But wisdom comes first in St. Paul's list of the Spirit's gifts, and that order may be intentional. I agree with the ancient church father Origen, who said wisdom may be the greatest and most beneficial gift. That's why I devoted an entire album called *Wisdom* to the topic.

Though I regularly ask the Spirit to grant me the gift of wisdom, it seems I typically receive only a drop of wisdom here, and a drop there; it's never a steady stream or a flood. But thankfully, a series of drops accumulated over a lifetime can fill a reservoir.

I have benefited greatly from other people who have received the gift of wisdom and freely shared it with me, occasionally changing my life in significant ways.

All wisdom ultimately comes from God, who gladly shares it with us, whether in drops or in floods. The Spirit's gift of wisdom can empower us to see and speak things human wisdom alone would never uncover.

WISDOM FOR THE COMMON GOOD

It can be challenging to distinguish wisdom from knowledge and prophecy, gifts that will be explored in later chapters.

St. Paul described both wisdom and knowledge as "words." The Spirit gives people these gifts so they will share words of wisdom with others. You and I may have personal wisdom or knowledge, but these gifts of the Spirit are given to us so that we may share them with others for their edification, as Paul told the church in Corinth:

> The manifestation of the Spirit is given for the common good.
> (1 Corinthians 12:7)

Both wisdom and knowledge are gifts that are given to be shared. But how are they different?

The Catholic Encyclopedia defines *wisdom* as "the grace of propounding the Faith effectively, of bringing home to the minds and hearts of the listener with Divine persuasiveness, the hidden mysteries and the moral precepts of Christianity."

- *Wisdom* helps believers understand the meaning of their faith and develop a personal system of ethics and morality they will live by. Words of wisdom often provide deeper insight into ordinary, external things of life.
- *Knowledge* typically focuses on interior, personal conditions. It is more intimate. When I meet with members of the community, I on occasion have been given special knowledge about their interior states.

Whenever I'm confronting decisions big or small, personal or in our community, I ask God for his wisdom.

MEET THE WORLD'S WISEST MAN

If the Psalms were Israel's hymnbook, Proverbs provided a handbook for practical living.

Modern readers may see Proverbs as a random collection of unrelated aphorisms, something like an ancient version of Benjamin Franklin's *Poor Richard's Almanac*. But the book is actually a guide prepared by ancient Jewish leaders to help people succeed in every area of life: relationships, family, work, business, ethics, government, and community.

The form of wisdom offered in Proverbs is extremely practical and earthy, not mystical, esoteric, or otherworldly.

These proverbs from numerous authors were collected and organized over centuries before being included in Scripture. Many are attributed to King Solomon, the son of King David, who reportedly spoke some three thousand wise sayings.

Solomon's story is told in the Old Testament book of 1 Kings, which describes how he received divine wisdom.

God appeared to Solomon one night in a dream and made a stunning offer: "Ask for whatever you want me to give you."

Solomon requested the gift he prized above all:

> Give your servant a discerning heart to govern your people and to distinguish between right and wrong.

God liked that answer!

> The Lord was pleased that Solomon had asked for this. So God said to him, "Since you have asked for this and not for long life or wealth for yourself, nor have asked for the death of your enemies but for discernment in administering justice, I will do what you have asked. I will give you a wise and discerning heart, so that there will never have been anyone like you, nor will there ever be.
>
> "Moreover, I will give you what you have not asked for— both wealth and honor—so that in your lifetime you will have no equal among kings. And if you walk in obedience to me and keep my decrees and commands as David your father did, I will give you a long life." (1 Kings 3:4–14)

Suppose you won the lottery, and now you had millions of dollars to spend on whatever possessions you wanted. Solomon faced a similar opportunity. He could have had whatever he wanted. He chose wisdom, and that choice should be a model for all of us. Too often, it seems, we seek other things that provide less payback than wisdom gives us.

God fulfilled his promises to make Solomon wise and wealthy, giving him "very great insight, and a breadth of understanding as measureless as the sand on the seashore. Solomon's wisdom was greater than the wisdom of all the people of the East, and greater than all the wisdom of Egypt. . . . And his fame spread to all the surrounding nations. . . . From all nations people came to listen to Solomon's wisdom, sent by all the kings of the world, who had heard of his wisdom" (1 Kings 4:29–34).

To see Solomon's wisdom in action, read about his most celebrated decision, a case where two women claimed the same child in 1 Kings 3:16–28.

YOUR WISDOM READING LIST

The Bible is full of wisdom, with much of it found in the five major wisdom books: Job, Proverbs, Ecclesiastes, Wisdom, and Sirach. These books were embraced by the early church, and they have been most enriching to me as I continue to seek out divine wisdom.

Each book is different. Job is an epic story. Ecclesiastes resembles Proverbs. Wisdom and Sirach are more orderly, addressing a variety of important topics, including advice on medicine, encouragement in facing death, and the theology of God's sovereignty and human free will.

At this point I can hear some of my Protestant friends saying, "Whoa! My Bible doesn't contain the books of Wisdom and Sirach." They are right. Protestant Bibles don't contain these two wisdom books, and that's too bad.

Originally these books were part of the Bible that Jews and the earliest Christians read. They are among the seven books called the deuterocanonical books, or as Protestants call them, the apocrypha.

Over the centuries, church councils decided which books would be included in the Christian Bible. Martin Luther and other European reformers deleted Wisdom and Sirach from Scripture, and Protestants have largely followed suit ever since. But now more Bible scholars and teachers from all Christian traditions are gradually adding these books to their approved reading lists.

If you desire wisdom, I recommend that you regularly study and reflect on these five books. (You can find them in Catholic Bibles, including the Revised Standard Version Catholic Edition, on the popular BibleGateway.com site.)

The book of Wisdom largely consists of couplets—which means two paired lines of poetry—that contrast goodness with evil, honesty with deceit, thrift with sloth. Similar contrasting couplets are found in the book of Proverbs:

> The path of the righteous is like the morning sun,
>> shining ever brighter till the full light of day.
> But the way of the wicked is like deep darkness;
>> they do not know what makes them stumble.
>
> (Proverbs 4:18–19)

I find that as I read and reread and reflect on these amazing books, God's wisdom is gradually etched in my brain.

One major theme of these books is that all of us should regularly seek God's wisdom, and that includes seeking the Spirit's gift of wisdom.

But there's no reason you and I should simply sit and wait on God to personally reveal his wisdom to each of us when he has abundantly revealed so much already in Scripture. It's our duty to study this wealth of wisdom God has made readily available to us.

As I was writing this book on the gifts of the Spirit, I regularly sought God's wisdom and guidance. But I didn't sit passively doing nothing until God supernaturally zapped me. Instead, I did my best to zealously study his Word and centuries' worth of wisdom from church fathers and other wise teachers.

I wrote a song called "I Sought the Lord" about our need to seek God's wisdom. I stole the lyrics from Ecclesiastes, but trust God won't sue for copyright infringement!

> I sought the Lord for Wisdom
> Therefore I prayed and prudence was given
> I preferred her to riches and gold
> In comparison with her all glory will fade
> Simply I learned of Wisdom
> Simply do I now share her with you
> She is an unfailing treasure
> And those who gain her win friendship with God

Do you desire God's wisdom? Then diligently seek it out. In my experience, people who truly desire wisdom and aggressively seek it out will find it, bit by bit.

TWO KINDS OF WISDOM

When I talk about wise people I don't mean "wise guys" like Tony Soprano and his criminal cronies from the popular *Sopranos* HBO series. Tony was definitely cunning in certain ways of the world, but he hardly qualified as wise.

Early in his letter to the Corinthians, Paul clearly contrasted two types of wisdom:

First, the person who is worldly wise:

Where is the wise person? Where is the teacher of the law? Where is the philosopher of this age? Has not God made foolish the wisdom of the world? (1 Corinthians 1:20)

Second, the person who has received God's wisdom:

We do, however, speak a message of wisdom among the mature, but not the wisdom of this age or of the rulers of this age, who are coming to nothing. (1 Corinthians 2:6)

Eugene Peterson's *The Message* puts it like this:

We, of course, have plenty of wisdom to pass on to you once you get your feet on firm spiritual ground, but it's not popular wisdom, the fashionable wisdom of high-priced experts that will be out-of-date in a year or so. God's wisdom is something mysterious that goes deep into the interior of his purposes. You don't find it lying around on the surface. It's not the latest message, but more like the oldest—what God determined as the way to bring out his best in us, long before we ever arrived on the scene. The experts of our day haven't a clue about what this eternal plan is. If they had, they wouldn't have killed [Jesus] on a cross. (1 Corinthians 2:6–9)

Christian philosopher and theologian St. Thomas Aquinas said believers make use of "two wisdoms . . . The uncreated wisdom of God and the created wisdom of man."[2]

Human wisdom has value, but all the human wisdom in the world will never reveal God to us. Divine wisdom flows from God.

The apostle James said that wisdom is a matter of the heart, not only the mind:

> Who is wise and understanding among you? Let them show it by their good life, by deeds done in the humility that comes from wisdom. But if you harbor bitter envy and selfish ambition in your hearts, do not boast about it or deny the truth. Such "wisdom" does not come down from heaven but is earthly, unspiritual, demonic. For where you have envy and selfish ambition, there you find disorder and every evil practice.
>
> But the wisdom that comes from heaven is first of all pure; then peace-loving, considerate, submissive, full of mercy and good fruit, impartial and sincere. (James 3:13–17)

Bottom line: Some people love wisdom and seek it out, while others run the other way:

> The fear [or overwhelming awe] of the LORD is the
> beginning of knowledge,
> but fools despise wisdom and instruction.
> (Proverbs 1:7)

WISE WORDS

When I was a baby Christian, I wanted to know God better. I was hungry for instruction, and my spiritual father, Father Martin, frequently gave me words of wisdom.

We would meet regularly, and I would pour out my heart

and all the questions on my mind. He would look at me as he listened intently, keeping silent for long periods of time. This silence seemed supernatural in itself, as Father Martin was usually quite talkative!

After a moment, he spoke, and his words carried power that pierced my heart. I felt like God himself was looking deep into my soul as Father Martin spoke. This was more than good advice. He was sharing the Spirit's gift with me through words of wisdom that seemed to come straight from God.

My song "Your Father's Teaching" offers a good description of how I felt:

> Happy the man who finds Wisdom
> Her profit is better than silver or gold
> When you are young, disdain not discipline
> And you'll be honored when you grow old

In general, I think it best to receive this kind of input from a trusted and proven spiritual guide whom you know well. But over the years, I have also received words of wisdom from friends, associates, complete strangers, and even some "fools for Christ."

I can remember times when I faced big decisions and, without providing details, asked friends to pray for me. At times, friends would approach me, tell me they believed they had received a word of wisdom for me in prayer, and ask me if I would be willing to hear it. After my consent, they shared words that gave me deep wisdom and accurate insights into the challenges I faced.

I've seen that God can offer words of wisdom through all kinds of people, regardless of their job titles, degrees, artfulness with language, or appearance. But others offered so-called words that never rang true. Such "words" should never be accepted without discernment.

WISDOM'S PARADOX

Some people say Christians are gullible goofballs who believe and do the silliest things.

They believe in a God who submitted to punishment on a cross, died, came back from the dead, and now answers billions of prayers.

They engage in cultish rituals like eating flesh and drinking blood.

They forgive cold-blooded murderers who entered their sacred assemblies and gunned down innocent worshippers and loved ones.

What fools!

St. Paul couldn't agree more.

For the message of the cross is foolishness to those who are perishing, but to us who are being saved it is the power of God. (1 Corinthians 1:18)

Paul's message was the inspiration for my song "The Cross Is Foolishness":

Some look for miracles, some look for wisdom
But we preach only Jesus crucified
It seems absurdity, it seems so foolish
But to us it is the wisdom of God

Welcome to the paradox of wisdom. A paradox is an apparent contradiction that somehow reveals a deeper, intuitive truth.

Paradox is mystery, the heart and goal of the way, truth, and life of Christ.

Christianity is full of paradoxes. Within our faith, we find:

- new life when we die to the old self through the cross of Christ,
- wealth in poverty,
- communion in solitude,
- freedom in obedience, and
- glory in humiliation.

Most major religions and philosophies embody some form of paradox, but Jesus is unique because he doesn't merely teach paradox; he is the incarnation of paradox. He is the Paradox of paradoxes, the man who was a God, the God who died, the God who rose from the dead.

Jesus was full of wisdom from an early age. While still a boy, he impressed Jewish teachers who were astonished at his understanding (Luke 2:47). Later during his public ministry, Jesus' preaching amazed people who asked, "Where did this man get this wisdom?" (Matthew 13:54).

Jesus embraced paradox throughout his public ministry, particularly in the Beatitudes portion of his sermon on the mount, which mirrors the contrasting couplets of Proverbs:

> Blessed are the poor in spirit,
>> for theirs is the kingdom of heaven.
> Blessed are those who mourn,
>> for they will be comforted.
> Blessed are the meek,
>> for they will inherit the earth. . . .

Blessed are those who are persecuted because of righteousness,
for theirs is the kingdom of heaven.

(Matthew 5:3–10)

In the centuries after Christ, a monk named Antony fled the civilized world to live the life of a hermit in the desert. Before long, he attracted thousands of other hermits and Christ-followers seeking silence and solitude. The collected sayings of these desert fathers were filled with paradox, and their pithy proverbs cross the centuries to speak to us today.

One of Antony's paradoxical proverbs went like this: "The prayer of the monk is not perfect until he no longer realizes himself or the fact that he is praying." Think about that for a moment and you will see that Antony is talking about a type of prayer in which one becomes lost in communion with the Father.

Another desert father said, "The man that every hour hath death before his eyes, will conquer meanness of soul." In other words, if you knew you were going to die tonight, maybe you would be kinder to the 7-Eleven clerk this afternoon.

St. Paul was a smart man who had been schooled in the same worldly wisdom and Jewish teaching he would later dismiss as foolishness. But Paul wasn't saying human wisdom is meaningless or evil. He was simply trying to remind us that human wisdom isn't wise enough on its own to lead us to God. That requires a higher, deeper wisdom.

For followers of Jesus, wisdom is found not through scholarship alone but through the paradox of the cross and the wisdom of God.

The foolishness of Christ doesn't mean that Christians are required to embrace crazy ideas, such as believing the earth is flat. But the foolishness of Christ does mean that you must place your life and your trust in him, which some people consider the height of foolishness.

MAKING LADY WISDOM YOUR FRIEND

Solomon does something interesting in Proverbs. He personifies wisdom, describing her as a woman:

> Does not wisdom call out?
>> Does not understanding raise her voice?
>>> (Proverbs 8:1).

The book of Wisdom (also known as the Wisdom of Solomon) does the same:

> Therefore I prayed, and understanding was given me;
>> I called on God, and the spirit of wisdom came to me.
>> I preferred her to scepters and thrones,
>> and I accounted wealth as nothing in comparison with her.
>>> (Wisdom 7:7–8 NRSV-CE)

The author went further, and described taking wisdom as a spouse:

> I loved her and sought her from my youth;
> I desired to take her for my bride.
>> (Wisdom 8:2 NRSV-CE)

This divine wisdom was the "secret sauce" that helped astronomers such as Copernicus, Kepler, Galileo, and Fr. Georges Lemaître radically change our understanding of creation.

Copernicus said the earth circled the sun at a time when the church taught otherwise. Kepler helped us understand that heavenly bodies travel in elliptical orbits. Galileo, who was more theologian, mystic, musician, and obedient son of the church than rebellious scientist, turned his telescope on the skies and described craters on the moon as well as moons around other planets. Similarly, Lemaître gave us the "Big Bang," which is the reigning scientific model for how the cosmos came to be.

But these discoveries weren't a result of any single man's wisdom; they were all because of God's wisdom:

> For it is he who gave me unerring knowledge of what
>   exists,
> to know the structure of the world and the activity of the
>   elements;
> the beginning and end and middle of times,
> the alternations of the solstices and the changes of the
>   seasons,
> the cycles of the year and the constellations of the stars.
>   (Wisdom 7:17–19 NRSV-CE)

There are two ways of knowing. One way is intellectual: 2 + 2 = 4. Another way to know is experiential and intuitive. That's the kind of knowledge you gain from knowing someone or something inside out. I can tell you what it's like to drive a car, but until you try it, you will never truly know.

God wants us to know wisdom intellectually *and* spiritually. He wants us to make her our friend, to marry her, to embrace her, to love her, to know her completely.

My song "Discipline (The Easy Yoke)" explains:

For her yoke is easy, her burden light
Take up your cross and follow
For her yoke is easy and her burden is light

HOW WISDOM WORKS WITHIN US

Wisdom has many characteristics and expresses herself in many ways. People occasionally ask me, "So, what is the primary characteristic of wisdom? How is wisdom manifested among us?"

I have reflected long and hard on this before concluding that wisdom is best seen in knowing when to be silent and when to speak, knowing when to be still and when to act, knowing when to humble yourself and when to be bold. This wisdom is so important that I wrote four songs about it on the *Wisdom* album.

The song "Humility" lays the foundation. If I'm not humble about the wisdom God gives me, I can make the mistake of thinking I'm pretty darn smart on my own.

The higher that you climb in life
Humble yourself all the more
You will be loved as a giver of gifts
You will find favor with God

The song "Swift to Hear, Slow to Answer" asks for divine help in taming the tongue. People love to talk, even when they have absolutely nothing to say. I want to be more like Father Martin: Listen much. Talk little.

Be swift to hear, slow to answer
A man's words can lead to his fall

If you have knowledge, humbly answer
If not, say nothing at all

When I do speak, I want to do so properly, speaking love and blessing, not anger and hate. The song "God Grant I Speak" can be sung as a prayer for those seeking to tame their own tongues:

God grant I speak suitably
We and our words are in his hand
He gives us knowledge of things that exist
The rules of the universe and the force of its elements

And if I find myself in those inevitable moments when I'm speaking too much or hurting others with my words, I need the song "Prayer":

Set a guard over my mouth
On my lips a sure seal
That I may not fall through my words
Let me speak only to heal
Apply the lash to my thoughts
To my mind the rod of discipline
For a word is the source of every deed
And the root of the words is the mind

For me it comes down to a few simple ideas. If you are afraid to be silent, then do not speak. If you are afraid to speak at the right time, then do not be silent. Ask God to give you the Spirit's gift of wisdom, then you can speak the right thing at the right time in a way that can truly build up and heal others.

ASK GOD

God seeks wise men and women. The world already has plenty of "wise guys."

Likewise, wise men and women seek God. They hunger for the Spirit's gift of wisdom. James told us how to ask: "If any of you lacks wisdom, you should ask God, who gives generously to all without finding fault, and it will be given to you" (James 1:5).

As you continue asking God for the gift of wisdom, make sure you do what James suggested in an earlier verse: "Let perseverance finish its work so that you may be mature and complete, not lacking anything" (v. 4). You can start by digging more deeply into some of the biblical wisdom books we explored in this chapter.

CHAPTER 5

THE GIFT OF KNOWLEDGE

THE INVISIBLE BECOMES VISIBLE

. . . a message of knowledge by
means of the same Spirit.
—1 CORINTHIANS 12:8

S he carried a heavy earthenware waterpot as she walked, her
eyes downcast. Her daily trip to fetch fresh water at the well
was planned for noontime, when few people ventured out into the
brutal heat. That way she would avoid people's taunts, condemn-
ing looks, and gossip.

Because it was the fastest route between Jerusalem and Galilee,
Jesus and his disciples were traveling through an area that many
travelers avoided. Samaria was a notorious hotbed of religious
cults and ethnic tensions. Although part of Israel, it was home
to altars of Baal and sites where pagans worshipped false gods.
Mainly, they accepted the five books of the Torah, but rejected

further revelation through the prophets or wisdom books. They were ancient fundamentalists! Righteous Jews were not to be seen near lowly Samaritans.

By noon, Jesus arrived at the well while his disciples went off to get some food. It was blisteringly hot, and he was thirsty. He asked the woman for a drink of water.

She nearly dropped her waterpot at the sound of his voice. Who was this man talking directly to her in this way? She could see Jesus was a Jew, making their presence here together not only a religious and cultural problem but also a possible sexual scandal.

"How is it that you, a Jew, ask for a drink from me, a woman of Samaria?"

It was a reasonable question. No Jewish man would want to be seen with a Samaritan woman, particularly *this* woman. As John told the story in the fourth chapter of his gospel, Jesus responded to the woman with a curious comment.

"If you knew the gift of God, and who it is that is saying to you, 'Give me a drink,' you would have asked him, and he would have given you living water."

The woman was confused. What was living water, and where was this man going to get it? He had no waterpot to suspend down into the well. Was he suffering from heat stroke? Did he think he was greater than the famous Jewish ancestor Jacob, who had drunk at this same well?

Jesus explained, "Everyone who drinks of this water will be thirsty again, but whoever drinks of the water that I will give him will never be thirsty again. The water that I will give him will become in him a spring of water welling up to eternal life."

That got her interested. She wanted to have the special water he offered so she wouldn't need to keep returning to the well every day. "Sir, give me this water, so that I will not be thirsty or have to come here to draw water."

That's when the conversation got even stranger. Jesus told her, "Go, call your husband, and come here."

"I have no husband," she replied.

"You are right in saying, 'I have no husband,'" Jesus answered. "The fact is, you have had five husbands, and the man you now have is not your husband. What you have just said is quite true."

Shocked, the woman suddenly understood what was happening.

"Sir," she said, "I perceive that you are a prophet."

In a moment, she would realize he was much more than a prophet. He was the promised Messiah. Jesus' knowledge of her life story was her first hint that something supernatural was going on here. She left her waterpot at the well and went to tell the townspeople.

> "Come, see a man who told me everything I ever did. Could this be the Messiah?" (John 4:29)

This is how the Spirit's gift of knowledge works. Invisible things become visible. Hidden things are brought into the open. Hurt and brokenness are exposed and revealed—not for purposes of shame and humiliation, but so people can experience healing, forgiveness, and salvation.

JESUS' KNOWLEDGE

The Spirit's gifts of words of knowledge and words of wisdom may seem similar, but as we said in the wisdom chapter, wisdom is often connected to exterior things, such as insight into living wisely in the messy world of daily life, or important decisions that need to be made about the direction of your life.

The Spirit's gift of knowledge is more about interior things, such as the state of the Samaritan woman's heart. Knowledge reveals secrets of the heart in a challenging but helpful way. In many later lives of the saints, such as the biography of St. Seraphim of Sarov, this is sometimes called insight.

Jesus was blessed with the Spirit's gift of knowledge. He could see into the woman's heart. He knew the deeper truth of the woman's story. This wasn't information he had gleaned while reading the latest issue of the *Samaria Journal*, or from searching the internet or social media posts. The truth of this woman's lonely life came directly from God.

Jesus exhibited the gift of knowledge throughout his ministry. Do you remember the story of the men who so desperately wanted Jesus to heal their paralyzed friend that they made a hole in the roof of the crowded house where he was teaching and lowered the man down into the room? Jesus healed the man and forgave his sins, which upset some teachers of religious law.

"Why does this fellow talk like that?" the teachers said to themselves. "He's blaspheming! Who can forgive sins but God alone?"

Jesus couldn't hear them talking, but he didn't need to. As Mark tells us, "immediately Jesus knew in his spirit that this was what they were thinking in their hearts, and he said to them, 'Why are you thinking these things?'" (Mark 2:1–8).

A similar scene accompanied another healing, this time in the Jewish synagogue.

"The Pharisees and the teachers of the law were looking for a reason to accuse Jesus, so they watched him closely to see if he would heal on the Sabbath." Jesus did heal on the Sabbath, but he knew the teachers were out to get him, so he outsmarted them (Luke 6:6–8).

Jesus gave his disciples wisdom as they traveled with him, talked with him, and heard him teach. "The knowledge of the secrets of the kingdom of God has been given to you," he told them, "but to others I speak in parables, so that, 'though seeing, they may not see; though hearing, they may not understand'" (Luke 8:10).

When Paul introduced the gifts of wisdom and knowledge to the church, he did so in the same brief sentence: "To one there is given through the Spirit a message of wisdom, to another a message of knowledge by means of the same Spirit" (1 Corinthians 12:8). This gift helped the early church preach, teach, and build strong communities of faith. Today, this gift helps us in similar ways, but it has been around for a long, long time.

OTHERS WHO KNOW

Have you ever heard the phrase "reading the writing on the wall"? This phrase comes from an amazing Old Testament story about Daniel, a Jewish hero who had been taken captive by Babylon's King Nebuchadnezzar. Nebuchadnezzar died, and now his son Belshazzar was on the Babylonian throne.

One night, Belshazzar threw a wild party where his guests used ceremonial goblets taken from the Jewish temple in Jerusalem to get drunk on wine while praising pagan gods. But everyone sobered up pretty quickly once a hand appeared and started writing on the wall.

The king summoned his "enchanters, astrologers and diviners," but none of these wise men of Babylon could read the writing on the wall. That's when the queen reminded the king about Daniel.

> Don't be alarmed! Don't look so pale! There is a man in your kingdom who has the spirit of the holy gods in him. In the time of your father he was found to have insight and intelligence and wisdom like that of the gods. . . . Daniel . . . was found to have a keen mind and knowledge and understanding, and also the ability to interpret dreams, explain riddles and solve difficult problems. Call for Daniel, and he will tell you what the writing means. (Daniel 5:10–12)

Daniel was summoned to read the writing, but his interpretation wasn't what the king had hoped for.

> You, Belshazzar, . . . have not humbled yourself. . . . Instead, you have set yourself up against the Lord of heaven. You had the goblets from his temple brought to you, and you and your nobles, your wives and your concubines drank wine from them. You praised the gods of silver and gold, of bronze, iron, wood and stone, which cannot see or hear or understand. But you did not honor the God who holds in his hand your life and all your ways. Therefore he sent the hand that wrote the inscription. (Daniel 5:22–24)

Daniel, who was blessed with the gifts of knowledge and prophecy, gave his interpretation of the writing on the wall. "You have been weighed on the scales and found wanting," he said. "God has numbered the days of your reign and brought it to an end" (Daniel 5:26–27).

As you can see for yourself by reading the fifth chapter of Daniel, Belshazzar died that very night.

Today, the gift of the word of knowledge remains active. For example, Padre Pio, the twentieth-century Italian saint who was famous for miracles, frequently exhibited the gift of knowledge. One website lists many examples.[1]

A woman came to visit the priest with her friends, but he said, "Why are you here? Go home, your husband is sick." The woman was surprised, because her husband had been perfectly healthy, but after quickly returning home, she found him in need of surgery.

Another time, he was approached by a man who "had the reputation of being a good Catholic, admired and esteemed by all who knew him." The man had come to the priest in confession saying he was dealing with a "spiritual crisis." But like Jesus at the well in Samaria, Padre Pio could tell there was more going on. The man had neglected his wife and was now in a relationship with another woman.

"What spiritual crisis?" demanded the priest, who could see the man's unconfessed sin. "God is angry with you. Go away!"

WORDS OF KNOWLEDGE

I wish I could exhibit the kind of knowledge that Jesus, Daniel, Padre Pio, and others have shown. On occasion I have personally experienced this gift, but typically I have been the person receiving the knowledge, not the one dispensing it.

In the previous chapter, I described how my spiritual father, Father Martin, frequently gave me words of wisdom during our long conversations. But it seems the words of knowledge I've received are more like quick blasts that have come from complete strangers or acquaintances I didn't know too well.

In some cases, I have received words of knowledge that felt like another person was granted temporary access to the deepest recesses of my soul. I can remember times of spiritual turmoil when humble souls who had my best interests at heart delivered words of knowledge that eased my worried heart and reassured me of God's love and care for me.

Some words I received seemed trivial. Others were most profound and benefitted me greatly. A few were downright earth shattering, and seemed truly born of God.

Twice I have even experienced "words" of knowledge that lacked words! This happened when I was introduced to two contemporary saints: Pope John Paul II and Teresa of Calcutta. In both cases, I was introduced to them briefly without either of us speaking anything but polite greetings, and in both cases, my innermost being was pierced with only a simple gaze.

I know I can't technically call the gifts I received in these two cases "words of knowledge," because not a word was spoken. But I sensed these two saints could see my soul when we met. It only took a moment, but it seemed an eternity, invading space and time and piercing my inner being.

I have also had bad experiences with so-called words of knowledge. After I entered the Catholic Church, you can bet I received so-called words of knowledge from angry Protestant friends claiming I was marrying "the whore of Babylon." Since then, people have given me "words" that were critical and extreme, such as claiming I wasn't really a follower of Jesus' will for my life. Some criticized my music and teaching ministry, some my vocation, and some my monastic marriage, which is part of church tradition but unusual to some today. Such criticism is part of public life. As they say, the higher the monkey climbs the tree, the more people criticize its backside!

I thank God that he protected me from these destructive words, because I've seen how sensitive souls can be led astray by authoritarian voices claiming a direct connection to God. Perhaps these are the kind of people Paul was describing when he said, "I can testify about them that they are zealous for God, but their zeal is not based on knowledge" (Romans 10:2).

Seldom have I been given a true word of knowledge. As we will see in chapter 10, "The Gift of Discerning Spirits," I more often have the ability to see the various spirits around a person. This "spiritual X-ray vision" vanishes within seconds, minutes, or hours, but these intuitions of spiritual states remain. I typically don't share these visions with people unless doing so would be edifying for them, but when I have done so they have checked out.

Only rarely have I felt that I was supposed to share that word or insight about a person's deepest secrets with them. That's due to my care and caution. I know that even the greatest knowledge, if shared unwisely, can cause great harm to another individual. So, when talking or meeting with either friends or community members, I keep my mouth shut so we can continue relating to each other or living together in community.

OUR KNOWLEDGE IS INCOMPLETE AND IMPERFECT

When there's a big political scandal in Washington, people ask:

What did he or she know?
And when did they know it?

Epistemology is a branch of philosophy that explores similar questions:

What do we really know?
And how do we know we know it?

St. Paul's discussion of spiritual gifts shows that our knowledge is partial at best.

We don't yet see things clearly. We're squinting in a fog, peering through a mist. But it won't be long before the weather clears and the sun shines bright! We'll see it all then, see it all as clearly as God sees us, knowing him directly just as he knows us! (1 Corinthians 13:12 THE MESSAGE)

Augustine wrote about the difficulty of knowing what we know more than fifteen centuries ago in his classic book *City of God*:

Our knowledge in this life remains imperfect, but it is reliable within its limits. Believers trust the witness of their senses, which are subservient to their intelligence. They may occasionally be deceived, but even so they are still better off than those who maintain that the senses can never be trusted.[2]

The bottom line here is that humility is essential when we talk about knowledge, whether human or divine. I may know a lot about church history, monastic life, or even theology, but I don't know everything, no matter how much I study. And even when God blesses me with his gift of knowledge, there are many topics where I remain ignorant.

There's another risk we need to watch out for: religious leaders and teachers who twist knowledge for their own power trips and selfish purposes. Jesus often condemned teachers of Jewish law who used their knowledge as a power to exclude others.

"Woe to you experts in the law, because you have taken away the key to knowledge. You yourselves have not entered, and you have hindered those who were entering" (Luke 11:52). And Paul warned against teachers "who worm their way into homes and gain control" over people's minds. Paul said these people had depraved minds, and I love his description of how they handle knowledge: "always learning but never able to come to a knowledge of the truth" (2 Timothy 3:6–7).

Bad teachers who twist God's truth are dangerous. In extreme cases, their claims to special, secretive knowledge of God's will can lead to tragedy. Jim Jones told his followers he knew God's truth, but more than nine hundred Jonestown residents committed suicide by drinking poison. In less extreme cases, bad teachers warp people's minds and close their hearts to the true knowledge of God's redeeming love.

We can use the minds God gave us to find some knowledge, and God may give us additional gifts of knowledge through his Spirit. But trouble is around the corner when you and I think and act as if we are much smarter than we really are. I try to remember: God knows everything. You and I know much, much less.

KNOWING BEYOND KNOWLEDGE

I have been married to a wonderful woman (and possible living saint!) named Viola for more than three decades. Much about our relationship is objective and knowable. We were married on a specific day in a specific place. We now live in an integrated monastic community in a particular location. Each one of us is of a specific age and has a particular height and weight. I know most of what she believes, likes, and wants. She is a serious charismatic Catholic Christian, likes flowers, and sometimes wants a frozen yogurt or ice cream. Facts are facts.

But much about our relationship is mysterious. She defies categorization and remains a delightful mystery to me! There are thoughts and emotions we share together that defy easy explanation. There's a closeness we share that enables us to anticipate each other's moods and attitudes, responses, and reactions. After years of constant contact and communication, there's a soul connection between us that goes beyond words and includes spirit, soul, and body.

Viola and I *know many facts* about each other. We also *know each other* in a deeper sense of husband and wife. We are best friends. These two ways of knowing also apply to our relationship with God. Many Christians know many facts about God, but God desires something deeper. He wants us to know him in a deeper way.

It is hard to describe this union with God, but I can show you what it looked like, at least to one famous sculptor. *The Ecstasy of St. Teresa* shows the sixteenth-century Spanish mystic Teresa of Ávila writhing, either in pain, bliss, or some overpowering combination of both. Teresa is portrayed in cold white marble that is polished to a brilliant sheen. Standing slightly above her is a smiling angel who holds a sharp pointed spear. And falling down upon them from heaven above are dozens of brilliant golden rays, symbolizing an overflowing of divine blessing.

The sculpture portrays a supernatural experience Teresa described in her autobiography, *The Interior Castle*:

I would see beside me . . . an angel in bodily form . . . He was
not tall, but short and very beautiful. In his hands I saw a long
golden spear and at the end of the iron top I seemed to see a point
of fire. With this he seemed to pierce my heart several times so
that it penetrated to my entrails. When he drew it out, I thought
he was drawing them out with it and he left me completely afire
with great love of God. The pain was so sharp that it made me
utter several moans; and so excessive was the sweetness caused
me by this intense pain that one can never wish to lose it, nor
will one's soul be content with anything less than God.[3]

Teresa even organized a marriage ceremony to celebrate her
spiritual marriage with God. "He must needs have an abiding-
place in the soul, just as He has one in Heaven, where His Majesty
alone dwells," she wrote. "So let us call this a second Heaven."[4]

Many mystics have used marriage as a metaphor to describe
their relationship with God. Jesus speaks of knowing God as a
deep knowing (γτνώσκω-*ginosko)*, similar to a man and woman
knowing each other in sexual union (Matthew 1:24). This gave
rise to the practice of spousal mysticism that sought such union
with God. You can see descriptions of spousal mysticism in the
works of St. Augustine, St. Bernard of Clairvaux, St. Bonaventure,
and St. John of the Cross. I authored my own book on this subject,
The Lover and the Beloved.

In the twentieth century, Thomas Merton described his experience near the end of his memoir, *The Seven Storey Mountain*,
writing that "the peak of the mystical life" was "a marriage of
the soul with God which gives the saints a miraculous power,
a smooth and tireless energy in working for God and for souls,
which bears fruits in the sanctity of thousands and changes the
course of religious and secular history."[5]

When you and I talk about knowing God, let's remember that "knowledge" means more than facts about God. It means knowing God himself, just as Jesus told the woman at the well: "God is spirit, and his worshipers must worship in the Spirit and in truth" (John 4:24).

PRACTICING THE GIFT OF KNOWLEDGE

St. Seraphim of Sarov reportedly lived such an exemplary life of humility and holiness that when he spoke, the first words from his mouth proved to be true words of knowledge, or as he called them, insights.

But without humility and holiness, such pronouncements can be false and destructive. That's why holiness and humility are spiritual prerequisites for exercising this powerful gift.

When you receive a supposed word of knowledge, you need to discern the truthfulness of the word with the help of your spiritual father or mother, or elders in the church. In my experience, words of knowledge and insights delivered by a trusted spiritual father, mother, or elder are the most reliable and safe.

Words of knowledge spoken to a person about something deep and intimate in their life and soul are not the same as human knowledge, but such words often include human wisdom.

Paul said the Spirit's gifts are for the common good, so a word of knowledge must be shared in great love and care for the genuine benefit of the other person. Knowledge isn't a means to judge or control others, but a gift designed to serve and love them. When used badly it can abuse their soul. When used well it is a wonderful gift.

That's why Paul prayed that believers would receive this gift:

For this reason, since the day we heard about you, we have not stopped praying for you. We continually ask God to fill you with the knowledge of his will through all the wisdom and understanding that the Spirit gives, so that you may live a life worthy of the Lord and please him in every way: bearing fruit in every good work, growing in the knowledge of God. (Colossians 1:9–10)

CHAPTER 6

THE GIFT OF FAITH

POWER TO BELIEVE

*Faith is confidence in what we hope for and
assurance about what we do not see.*

—HEBREWS 11:1

It was Easter morning 2019, and thousands of believers packed into churches across Sri Lanka. That's when suicide bombers struck, killing more than 250 people in coordinated attacks in the cities of Colombo, Negombo, and Batticaloa.

The following Sunday, many surviving believers hoped to return to their badly destroyed churches to worship. But bishops cancelled Sunday Masses due to threats of new attacks and instead shared a worship service via online video.

Son Jong-nam defected from North Korea to China, then he returned to his home country with Bibles and cassette tapes to help him proclaim the gospel. He was arrested in 2006 and charged with illegally crossing a border, meeting with enemies of the state, and disseminating anti-state literature.

After North Korean leaders announced that Son would be publicly executed, international pressure changed their plans. Son's brother believes they quietly tortured him to death in a Pyongyang prison, where he died in 2008.

Gayle Williams served at a Christian ministry in Afghanistan, helping children who were deaf, blind, disabled, or injured due to warfare and landmines. She was careful not to convert Muslims, which would anger the Taliban.

In 2008, she attended the funeral of a colleague at Kabul cemetery, where she told a coworker that if she were killed, she would like to be buried in the same cemetery. A few weeks later she was shot on her way to work by two men on a motorbike.

FAITH THAT TRUSTS GOD

These brave souls had faith in God, the kind of unshakable faith in an all-powerful God that allowed them to totally entrust their lives to his care as they ministered in his name, no matter the dangers they faced.

Stories of faith in the face of harassment, persecution, and death are nothing new. Jesus warned his disciples they would be betrayed, arrested, hated, flogged, and killed—all because they followed him.

He was right. Within decades of Christ's crucifixion, Peter, Paul, Stephen, and three disciples named James were martyred for their faith. Other followers were beheaded, crucified, and thrown to the lions in the Roman Colosseum. By the second century, early church father Tertullian would write: "The blood of the martyrs is the seed of the Church." That has proven to be true.

Jesus warned his followers of the trials to come, but he also called them to persevere despite the risk.

> Do not be afraid of those who kill the body but cannot kill the soul. Rather, be afraid of the One who can destroy both soul and body in hell. . . . Whoever acknowledges me before others, I will also acknowledge before my Father in heaven. (Matthew 10:28, 32)

Gayle Williams had this kind of faith. At her colleague's funeral, she told a friend, "These bodies are only temporary. When I get to heaven I will have a new body."

Do you have this kind of faith in God?

Do I have this kind of faith?

While it is true that I have repeatedly "acknowledged" Christ before many other people, I typically do so when I'm singing or speaking at Christian concerts or ministries. I have seldom faced threats of persecution or death for singing my songs or teaching. Opposition has happened on rare occasion, and it is only by God's grace that I have been able to respond calmly and peacefully.

Would I boldly proclaim Christ if I knew that persecution or torture would surely follow rather than applause and a stipend? I pray that I would, but I'm really not sure I have that kind of faith.

Faith is at the core of the Christian life, but Paul said there was a special kind of faith that came as a gift of the Holy Spirit: "To one there is given through the Spirit a message of wisdom, to another a message of knowledge by means of the same Spirit, *to another faith* by the same Spirit" (1 Corinthians 12:8–9, emphasis added).

Christians have embraced this supernatural gift of faith for centuries. Cyril of Jerusalem was a fourth-century church father who is embraced as a saint by Catholic, Orthodox, and Anglican Christians. He described this special gift in his classic work, the *Catechetical Lectures*:

> As a noun the word faith is but one; yet, its meaning is twofold. There is the one kind, dogmatic faith, involving assent of the soul to something or other; and it is profitable to the soul . . . But there is a second kind of faith, which is given by Christ as a kind of grace . . . This faith which is given by the Spirit as a grace is not just doctrinal faith but a faith which empowers activities surpassing human nature, a faith which moves mountains.[1]

The thousands of Christian martyrs who die for their faith every year need this kind of faith. So do ordinary, nonheroic believers like you and me, whose worst problems are traffic jams or disobedient kids.

We need faith because we are living in an age of pragmatism and skepticism, a time when belief is ridiculed and dismissed.

As previously mentioned, the fastest-growing "religious" group in America today is "nones"—people professing no religious faith affiliation. Many "nones" seem to be "dones." They may have been practicing Christians at one time, but now they've simply had it with any kind of organized religion. They're done with it.

Religious sex scandals, financial scams, and polarized and hate-filled politics have eroded the moral authority of Christians of all traditions—Catholic, Protestant, Orthodox, Anglican, evangelical.

Clearly, we need the Spirit's supernatural gift of faith today.

FAITH'S FOUNDATIONS

Our world has seen its share of gurus and holy men, but Jesus was different. He was more than a teacher or preacher. He was the Christ, the Son of God. He was both human and divine. And three days after his public crucifixion, he rose from the dead and appeared to his disciples, just as he had foretold.

Being Christian doesn't mean you have faith in *faith*. It's not *faith* that saves us, but only Christ. Faith that is Christian is founded upon belief in Christ's divinity, his resurrection, his love and forgiveness, and his ongoing presence in our lives.

The New Testament spells out some essentials of Christian faith:

- "For we live by faith, not by sight" (2 Corinthians 5:7).
- "Faith comes from hearing the message, and the message is heard through the word about Christ" (Romans 10:17).
- "If Christ has not been raised, your faith is futile; you are still in your sins. Then those also who have fallen asleep in Christ are lost. If only for this life we have hope in Christ, we are of all people most to be pitied" (1 Corinthians 15:17–19).
- "Now faith is confidence in what we hope for and assurance about what we do not see" (Hebrews 11:1). The word translated as "confidence" (or "substance") is the Greek ὑ of thin-*hypostasis*, which can also mean "person." Church fathers used this word for the persons of the Trinity, or the union of divinity and humanity in the one person of Jesus.

So, faith actually personifies *now* the good things we hope for *tomorrow*.

Faith does not mean "believing something you know ain't true," as Mark Twain put it in his 1897 book *Following the Equator*. But it does involve believing in things we cannot yet see—things some people think are crazy or foolish.

I think St. Augustine struck the right balance. "I believe, in order to understand; and I understand, the better to believe" (Sermon 43:9).

FIGHTING OVER FAITH

For centuries, Christians have argued about faith versus works. Each of the two sides has its favorite Bible verses.

"Faith Alone" Side

FAVORITE VERSES: "For it is by grace you have been saved, through faith—and this is not from yourselves, it is the gift of God—not by works, so that no one can boast" (Ephesians 2:8–9).

"Faith Plus" Side

FAVORITE VERSES: "What good is it, my brothers and sisters, if someone claims to have faith but has no deeds? Can such faith save them? . . . As the body without the spirit is dead, so faith without deeds is dead" (James 2:14, 26).

Martin Luther was a Catholic monk who launched the Protestant Reformation that broke away from the Catholic Church. Luther thought Catholics had an overly works-oriented view of salvation that gave rise to various abuses.

Luther was reacting to those in the church who falsely promised that people could escape purgatory by buying indulgences to finance the construction of St. Peter's Basilica in Rome, or that people could earn heavenly bonus points by merely putting themselves through all kinds of repetitive, external rituals and self-punishment without understanding their real meaning.

While Luther had a good point about the danger of believing that your own works can earn your salvation, I think he took things too far, and his "reform" ended up splintering Christianity in the West far beyond his original intent.

Overall, the whole faith-versus-works debate is a false dichotomy, as we saw in 1999, when the Catholic Church and the Lutheran World Federation signed a "Joint Declaration on the Doctrine of Justification" that said people in the two faith traditions now shared "a common understanding of our justification by God's grace through faith in Christ."[2]

Here's a balanced perspective for understanding faith and works:

- We are saved by grace, which is an unmerited gift from God.
- Grace gives birth to faith.
- Faith gives birth to good works.

The modern-day martyrs we met in the beginning of the chapter didn't merely have faith; they took action based on their faith. I believe God's Spirit gave them a special gift of faith that empowered them to love God, serve their neighbors, and face the horrors they faced every day.

BETWEEN FAITH AND DOUBT

One day, Jesus' disciples tried but failed to cast a demon out of a boy, so Jesus cast out the demon. The disciples asked Jesus why they had failed.

"Because you have so little faith," Jesus replied. "Truly I tell you, if you have faith as small as a mustard seed, you can say to this mountain, 'Move from here to there,' and it will move. Nothing will be impossible for you" (Matthew 17:20).

We must dare to believe with faith what we are asking for, or it won't happen. This is the faith that moves mountains. We must expect a miracle when we pray by faith. This takes boldness! But we must also humbly accept the miracle he gives by faith.

The Bible contains many powerful stories about faith, but it also shows what can happen when faith fails. All of us struggle with doubt from time to time, but few of us have failed as spectacularly and as publicly as Peter, who was one of Jesus' more colorful and complicated disciples. Two stories from the New Testament illustrate his struggles.

In one case, Jesus was walking on the water when Peter decided he would like to try water-walking himself (Matthew 14:22–33). It went fine for a while, with Peter making uneven progress on the heaving surface of a lake. Then his doubts tripped him up:

> "When he saw the wind, he was afraid and, beginning to sink, cried out, "Lord, save me!"
>
> Immediately Jesus reached out his hand and caught him. "You of little faith," he said, "why did you doubt?" (vv. 30–31)

After this comical episode, Peter's next failure of faith was sad to see. Jesus was soon to be arrested and crucified, and after he and his disciples shared their last supper, Jesus said, "This very night you will all fall away on account of me."

Peter replied, "Even if all fall away on account of you, I never will."

"Truly I tell you," Jesus answered, "this very night, before the rooster crows, you will disown me three times."

Peter wasn't having it. "Even if I have to die with you, I will never disown you," Peter insisted.

A short time later, after Jesus had been arrested, three different people asked Peter if he knew Jesus. After assuring all three people that he didn't know Jesus, a rooster crowed. Peter suddenly remembered Jesus' prediction about his faithlessness and "wept bitterly" (Matthew 26:31–35, 69–74).

Thankfully, that is not the end of the story. After Christ's resurrection, Peter emerged as one of the strongest and boldest of the apostles. He repeatedly risked his life and safety to proclaim the gospel and was ultimately crucified for his faith during Nero's bloody persecution, which ran from AD 64 to 67. Peter requested that he be crucified upside down because he felt unworthy to die as Christ had died.

Peter's struggles with faith provide powerful lessons:

- Even a weak faith in a strong God can be a powerful thing.
- Even when you and I may be weak and conflicted, God remains steadfast and loving.
- Even a failed faith can be restored through God's grace.

I find that very encouraging. I hope you do too.

WHEN FAITH GETS CRAZY

They are all over television and the internet: prosperity preachers who promise viewers that faith in God—combined with a generous contribution to the preacher—will automatically result in improved physical and mental health, better marriages, and vast windfalls of money.

Their teaching is loosely based on a powerful promise from Jesus: "Therefore I tell you, whatever you ask for in prayer, believe that you have received it, and it will be yours" (Mark 11:24).

What prosperity preachers often forget to mention is that while God answers prayers, he often does so in ways we never expected. It's one thing to go to God in prayer demanding twenty-five thousand dollars. It's a completely different thing to pray to God with open hands and an open heart, expectantly receiving whatever gift he chooses to give us.

I tried to paint a picture of this kind of humble, open-handed faith in the song "Before the Father":

I kneel before the Father
From whom every family in heaven and on earth takes its name
And I pray He will bestow
Gifts in keeping with the riches of His Glory
May He strengthen you inwardly
Through the working of His Spirit
May Christ dwell within your heart through faith
And may charity be the root and sure foundation of your life
And so attain unto the fullness of God Himself
And may you grasp fully with all of the holy ones
Who have surely come before
The height and depth and the width and breadth of Christ's love

And experience this love beyond knowledge
May He strengthen you inwardly
Through the working of His Spirit
May Christ dwell within your heart through faith
And may charity be the root and sure foundation of your life
And so attain unto the fullness of God Himself
I kneel before the Father
From whom every family in heaven and on earth takes its name

But unfortunately the "name-it-and-claim-it" folks aren't the only Christians giving faith a bad name. I have experienced way too many cases of faith-based weirdness. I've seen people doing really far-out things in the name of faith, and these excesses have hurt many innocent bystanders.

I've lost count of the times people proclaimed a "word of faith" straight from God that the apocalypse is coming and the world will end the next day, week, month, or year. (This may actually qualify as false prophecy.)

I have seen people go into deep debt based on faith that God will protect them from their disastrous financial decisions. I have seen people cite faith as their reason for avoiding doctors, dentists, or vaccinations, a practice that was criticized in the deuterocanonical book of Sirach, which says, "He who sins against his Maker, will be defiant toward the physician" (38:15 NRSV-CE).

I have also been involved in two difficult concert situations where artists decided on faith to violate the terms of their contracts. In one case, my brother Terry and I were on the same bill with headliner Barry McGuire and a third artist who was to perform a brief opening set. But somewhere along the line, this third musician came to believe that God wanted him to play the whole concert by himself, and that's exactly what he did, performing for three hours straight and preventing me, Terry, and Barry from singing for the people who had come to see us.

FAITH IS A GIFT WE NEED

Around the world, men and women are exhibiting a supernatural faith.

Ragheed Ganni was born in Iraq. After studying in Rome, he asked to be sent back to Iraq to work as a Catholic priest. Father Ganni served the Holy Spirit Chaldean Church in Mosul, where his three cousins served as deacons.

One night after Mass, a man approached them making demands: the four Catholic leaders were to forsake their faith in Christ, convert to Islam, and shut down the church.

"How can I close the house of God?" Father Ganni asked.

The four men were shot and killed in 2007, and their bodies were loaded into a car full of explosives, threatening anyone wanting to retrieve their bodies.

You can learn more about the ministry of modern-day martyrs by following the work of ministries such as Open Doors or Voice of the Martyrs. Meanwhile, you can ask God for the gift that empowers you to face your world with a supernatural faith.

I know faith can be abused. I've seen how we can put our faith in things that don't deserve it. On the other hand, there are many godly institutions that need our support.

I have great faith in God's universal church, even when she falls into money, sex, and power scandals. The Catholic Church has struggled with sex scandals for years, but we're not the only ones. Bill Hybels, founder of the influential Willow Creek Community Church in Illinois, which once boasted twenty-four thousand members, and the Willow Creek Association, which was joined by more than five thousand individual evangelical congregations, stepped down in 2018 after long-simmering accusations were confirmed. And in 2019, the *Houston Chronicle* reported that Southern Baptist churches were home to nearly four hundred leaders and volunteers who had abused more than seven hundred victims.

God has protected and guided his church for nearly two thousand years, and I believe he will continue to do so.

I have great faith in the monastic calling, even though few even consider it an option in today's secularized culture.

I have faith in the charismatic expressions of the church, even when I see some of the gifts dying out in the Western world because we are too darn rational.

I have faith in God's mercy and forgiveness even though I am living in a divisive and judgmental society.

I have faith in healing the sick, even when death seems inevitable.

As I said, I don't believe God has given me an extraordinary gift of faith, even though there are times when my sudden expressions of faith surprise me. But I am certainly open to this gift and continue to pray for it.

I recommend you pray for the gift of faith that can help you believe all things are possible with God.

CHAPTER 7

THE GIFT OF HEALING

DIVINE POWER FOR BODY, SOUL, AND SPIRIT

Jesus went throughout Galilee, teaching in their
synagogues, proclaiming the good news of the kingdom,
and healing every disease and sickness among the people.
—MATTHEW 4:23

I saw it myself, and it astonished me! Right there, before my very eyes, and the eyes of a dozen other people, the woman's leg grew three inches longer.

It was the early 1990s, and I was a member of one of many small teams of believers working with a Catholic priest blessed with the Spirit's gift of healing. We were at a big charismatic conference in St. Louis, and teams were praying for people all over the large auditorium.

The priest's official name was Rev. Paul Robert DeGrandis, SSJ, but we simply called him "Father Bob."

There was nothing extraordinary about Father Bob, and when I hung around with him, he was just an ordinary guy. But this ordinary guy was blessed with an extraordinary gift: the Holy Spirit's gift of healing. From 1979 to the time he died in 2018, Father Bob was ordained to full-time ministry serving the Catholic charismatic renewal community throughout America and in thirty-five countries around the world.

Father Bob was leading the conference in St. Louis where I saw the healing take place. I was with about a dozen fellow believers who stood around a woman, praying for God to heal her leg. As we prayed together, we saw her leg transformed. I was stunned to see this supernatural gift exhibited so clearly in our presence, but I can't say it totally surprised me. That's because I believe that the Holy Spirit has often given people the gift of healing over the past two thousand years.

As thrilling as it was to participate in miraculous healings with other believers, it seems God has so far declined to give me the gift of healing another person.

Over the years, people have told me they've experienced various forms of healing through my ministry of music, teaching, and writing. But this doesn't mean I have received the Spirit's gift of healing.

Rather, this shows that God is gracious to work in and through any believer who devotes him- or herself to God's service and serves as an open and willing channel for the Spirit to pass through.

OUR CREATOR IS A HEALER

God has been healing his people from the beginning of time, as we see throughout Scripture and history.

JEWISH SCRIPTURES

Supernatural healings are described in the Law and the Prophets. For example, the fifth chapter of 2 Kings gives a lengthy report on how Elisha healed Naaman of leprosy in the Jordan River.

JESUS

Many people think of Jesus as a wonderful teacher, and he was. He was also a healer, and his many recorded miraculous healings demonstrated God's miraculous powers and liberated people from the destructive effects of sin and alienation from God.

The Gospels show how Jesus' teaching and healing ministries were linked: "Jesus went throughout Galilee, teaching in their synagogues, proclaiming the good news of the kingdom, and healing every disease and sickness among the people" (Matthew 4:23).

John reports that Jesus' healing miracles made him a regional celebrity who drew crowds hungry for more miracles: "and a great crowd of people followed him because they saw the signs he had performed by healing the sick" (John 6:2).

Matthew shows that even when Jesus tried to get a moment away from the crowds and pray to his Father, the crowds came, and he welcomed them. After Jesus withdrew from the crowds in one place, "a large crowd followed him, and he healed all who were ill" (Matthew 12:10–15).

Jesus even healed on the Sabbath, which brought predictable condemnation from the religious legalists of his day (Matthew 12:10).

Jesus healed for various reasons. Sometimes he healed because of the faith of the sick person (Matthew 9:28) and sometimes because of the faith of other people (Mark 2:5). In some cases,

Jesus healed to manifest the supernatural power of God. That's what happened in perhaps Jesus' most stunning miraculous healing: the raising of his friend Lazarus from the dead.

"It is for God's glory so that God's Son may be glorified through it" (John 11:1–4).

We explored Jesus' healing of the paralytic man in chapter 5, but this chapter also shows that Jesus healed people's bodies to demonstrate that he could also heal their souls and forgive their sins. Jesus responded to the strong faith of the four men who lowered the paralytic man into the room where he was teaching (Mark 2:3–12).

"When Jesus saw their faith, he said to the paralyzed man, 'Son, your sins are forgiven'" (v. 5).

After teachers of the law accused him of blaspheming, he responded:

> Why are you thinking these things? Which is easier: to say to this paralyzed man, "Your sins are forgiven," or to say, "Get up, take your mat and walk"? But I want you to know that the Son of Man has authority on earth to forgive sins. So he said to the man, "I tell you, get up, take your mat and go home." He got up, took his mat and walked out in full view of them all. This amazed everyone and they praised God, saying, "We have never seen anything like this!" (vv. 8–12)

APOSTLES

Jesus' apostles were empowered with the gift of supernatural healing: "Jesus called his twelve disciples to him and gave them authority to drive out impure spirits and to heal every disease and sickness" (Matthew 10:1).

The apostles frequently used this gift, as we see throughout the book of Acts. In one case (Acts 3:1–10), a man approached Peter and John seeking money from the famous miracle workers:

> Peter looked straight at him, as did John. . . . Then Peter said, "Silver or gold I do not have, but what I do have I give you. In the name of Jesus Christ of Nazareth, walk." Taking him by the right hand, he helped him up, and instantly the man's feet and ankles became strong. He jumped to his feet and began to walk. Then he went with them into the temple courts, walking and jumping, and praising God. (vv. 4–8)

The apostles performed so many signs and wonders that they, too, became famous and attracted followers (Acts 5:12–16). "People brought the sick into the streets and laid them on beds and mats so that at least Peter's shadow might fall on some of them as he passed by" (v. 15).

CHURCH HISTORY

After the Holy Spirit appeared in power on the day of Pentecost, the Spirit distributed the healing gift to members of the church, as Paul described:

> To one there is given through the Spirit a message of wisdom, to another a message of knowledge by means of the same Spirit, to another faith by the same Spirit, to another gifts of healing by that one Spirit. (1 Corinthians 12:8–9)

Healing has played a significant role in the life of the church whenever Christians have devoted themselves to healing through both supernatural and medical means. You can see healings reported in the lives of many saints. The biography of St. Antony of the Desert reveals a heavy reliance on miracle stories and the gift of healing. The biographies of St. Benedict and St. Francis of Assisi include healing miracles. Today, healing miracles are often cited in the process of canonizing saints.

A brief stroll through later chapters of church history shows that healing was important to many prominent leaders and movements:

- Quaker founder *George Fox* promoted both the gift of healing and the ministry of doctors.
- *Ellen Gould White*, cofounder of the Seventh-day Adventists, practiced the gift of healing and combined this with teaching on healthy living, which remains an Adventist distinctive today.
- *Johann Christoph Blumhardt* was a nineteenth-century German Lutheran pastor who, after a battle with the Devil, inspired a revival in his parish that included both physical healings and radical life transformation.
- *Dorothea Trudel* was a Swiss healer who won court decisions allowing her to continue her work.
- *Otto Stockmayer* inspired a healing revival in Europe, and his work with England's Keswick holiness movement led to speaking tours in Britain and the United States.
- In the 1940s and '50s, a healing revival spread throughout Pentecostal churches, introducing Americans to *Oral Roberts*, who founded Oral Roberts University.
- And in the 1960s and '70s, members of the Jesus movement and charismatic movement witnessed healing miracles in their midst.

Throughout history, there have been both sincere Christians with the gift of supernatural healing, as well as con men and hucksters who perform cheap parlor tricks to exploit people's hunger for the miraculous. Believers must be discerning, but we shouldn't allow fakes or flim-flam to make us doubt God's healing powers.

HEALING: MIRACULOUS OR MEDICAL?

People occasionally ask me for advice, saying they were experiencing physical ailments but didn't know whether to pray to God or go to a doctor.

"Yes," I always tell them, "do both. Pray to God for healing, and go to a doctor to see if this physician is the human agent through whom God desires to heal you."

We know that Luke the apostle was a doctor (Colossians 4:14) who made use of both natural and supernatural healing. Since then, Christianity has had a twenty-century-long tradition of combining spiritual and medical healing.

"Christianity planted the hospital," wrote historian Roy Porter in his nearly nine-hundred-page book *The Greatest Benefit to Mankind: A Medical History of Humanity*.[1] The world's first hospitals were founded by Christians, and one of the earliest was St. Basil's great fourth-century Basiliad. This wonder of the ancient world, where monastics ministered to the sick, was the first major Christian hospital and educational facility the world had yet seen.

The earliest hospitals in America were founded by Catholic sisters, and these hospitals served Catholics, non-Catholics, and atheists alike. Today, many hospitals and hospital systems are operated by Catholics, Adventists, Presbyterians, and other people of faith.

One hallmark of global Christian missionaries is the establishment of mission hospitals that serve millions of people throughout the developing world. Our group, the Brothers and Sisters of Charity, founded the first free clinic in our area of the Arkansas Ozarks. And when we opened a mission on the island of Ometepe in Nicaragua, we founded the first clinic on the southern half of the island, which had previously not enjoyed good medical care.

This tradition of seeking the best of medical and spiritual healing dates back centuries before Christ, as we see in the book of Sirach, which says we are to honor God and seek healing from him, but we should also seek God's healing through doctors:

> Honor physicians for their services,
>> for the Lord created them;
> for their gift of healing comes from the Most High,
>> and they are rewarded by the king.
> The skill of physicians makes them distinguished,
>> and in the presence of the great they are admired.
> The Lord created medicines out of the earth,
>> and the sensible will not despise them.
> Was not water made sweet with a tree
>> in order that its power might be known?
> And he gave skill to human beings
>> that he might be glorified in his marvelous works.
> By them the physician heals and takes away pain;
>> the pharmacist makes a mixture from them.
> God's works will never be finished;
>> and from him health spreads over all the earth.

Long before I ever advised people to pray for healing *and* go to a doctor, Sirach offered similar advice:

My child, when you are ill, do not delay,
  but pray to the Lord, and he will heal you.
Give up your faults and direct your hands rightly,
  and cleanse your heart from all sin.
Offer a sweet-smelling sacrifice, and a memorial portion of
  choice flour,
  and pour oil on your offering, as much as you can afford.
Then give the physician his place, for the Lord created him;
  do not let him leave you, for you need him.
There may come a time when recovery lies in the hands of
  physicians,
  for they too pray to the Lord
that he grant them success in diagnosis
  and in healing, for the sake of preserving life.
He who sins against his Maker,
  will be defiant toward the physician.

(Sirach 38:1–15 NRSV-CE)

This Scripture passage shows the perfect balance between divine healing and good medical practices. We need both kinds of healing. God heals, but not every time we're sick. Doctors heal, but their healing is often incomplete, and can even be downright harmful.

In 1957, doctors prescribed a new drug called thalidomide to pregnant women dealing with morning sickness. Over the next four years, some ten thousand babies were born with severe birth defects, and some two thousand babies died.

In our own day, we've also seen how medicine can kill. In 2017 alone, nearly fifty thousand Americans died from overdosing on opioids.

Today, people complain about rising medical costs, but

frustration with medical professionals is nothing new. One day a woman approached Jesus after experiencing years of medical problems (Mark 5:25–34): "a woman was there who had been subject to bleeding for twelve years. She had suffered a great deal under the care of many doctors and had spent all she had, yet instead of getting better she grew worse" (vv. 25–26).

But when she touched Jesus' cloak, she experienced immediate healing. "Daughter," Jesus told her, "your faith has healed you. Go in peace and be freed from your suffering" (v. 34).

DIVINE HEALING: PHYSICAL, SPIRITUAL, EMOTIONAL, OR MENTAL?

God created us with bodies and spirits, minds and emotions. Each part of us can become broken or sick, but thank God because he heals all our parts. The word the New Testament uses to describe Jesus' healing ministry is θεραπεύω (*therapeuo* /ther·ap·yoo·o/), which is where we get our English word *therapy*.

God wants to heal us from whatever ails us. That's good, because most of us need healing of one kind or another:

- Our need for healing might be physical, because of an illness, an injury, or disease.
- For many of us, sickness resides in our thoughts, which can follow negative and destructive patterns.
- Some of us experience emotional illness due to abuse, shock, trauma, or the basic challenges of everyday life.
- And I have seen people experience spiritual harm after being abused by destructive, cultic spiritual groups and gurus.

In recent decades, science has shown us more evidence about the powerful connection between body, mind, and spirit. All are related, and each impacts the other. Negative thoughts and feelings can result in physical manifestations or psychosomatic illness.

I know God is a healer, so I ask him for healing no matter whether I'm suffering in my spirit, mind, or emotions. I tried to express this desire for God to heal me of everything all the time in the song "Healer of My Soul":

Healer of my soul
Keep me at even
Keep me at morning
Keep me at noon
Healer of my soul
Keeper of my soul
On rough course faring
Help and safeguard my means this night
Keeper of my soul
I am tired, astray, and stumbling
Shield my soul from the snare of sin
Healer of my soul
Heal me at even
Heal me at morning
Heal me at noon
Healer of my soul

THE FAITH PRESCRIPTION

When people approached Jesus to request healing, he often asked two questions:

- Do you want to be healed? (John 5:6)
- Do you have faith that God can heal you? (Matthew 9:28)

When I look at healing accounts in the Bible, as well as the healings I have witnessed myself, it seems that we need the gift of faith to appropriate the gift of healing. The Gospels show that one man had this kind of faith, even though he was not Jewish, while others lacked such faith.

Jesus was approached by a centurion, an officer in the Roman army, but the man turned down Jesus' request to follow him home and heal his servant there.

> Lord, I do not deserve to have you come under my roof. But just say the word, and my servant will be healed. For I myself am a man under authority, with soldiers under me. I tell this one, "Go," and he goes; and that one, "Come," and he comes. I say to my servant, "Do this," and he does it. (Matthew 8:8–9)

Jesus responded: "Truly I tell you, I have not found anyone in Israel with such great faith." The centurion's servant "was healed at that moment" (Matthew 8:10–13).

Faith was lacking in other cases, and that faithlessness hindered healing. Jesus' own disciples failed to heal a man's son who suffered from seizures, requiring Jesus to heal the son himself by driving out a demon who had afflicted the boy.

Later, his disciples asked him, "Why couldn't we drive it out?"

"Because you have so little faith," he replied (Matthew 17:15–20).

Even Jesus experienced an inability to work miracles, except for a few healings, when people in his hometown doubted his divinity. "He was amazed at their lack of faith" (Mark 6:4–6).

When you ask God to heal you, do so with faith, believing that he will respond, and embrace his response.

SEEKING GOD'S HEALING

Are you sick or troubled? Do you need healing? James urged us to make our request to God:

> Is anyone among you in trouble? Let them pray. Is anyone happy? Let them sing songs of praise. Is anyone among you sick? Let them call the elders of the church to pray over them and anoint them with oil in the name of the Lord. And the prayer offered in faith will make the sick person well; the Lord will raise them up. If they have sinned, they will be forgiven. Therefore confess your sins to each other and pray for each other so that you may be healed. The prayer of a righteous person is powerful and effective. (James 5:13–16)

Like Jesus, James connected physical healing to spiritual healing. For the sick person to become truly well, body and spirit should be healed.

I've seen the gift of healing manifested during the Catholic sacrament of healing, a ritual through which people pray for the sick. In the Catholic Church, gifts of the Spirit are sometimes institutionalized in sacraments that millions of believers participate in. Meanwhile, mystics and saints have continued to demonstrate the ability to heal outside of the normal sacramental means.

Unfortunately, too many people are doubtful that God can heal anyone. I saw this for myself at a convention of the Southern

California Renewal Communities, which sponsors the largest charismatic conference in the United States.

I was one of many presenters there. After I sang and gave a talk on healing, I went to an assigned station to greet and pray with people. A long line of several hundred formed, and many asked for healing, but there was a skepticism in their requests.

"I know Jesus won't heal my cancer," one told me, "but I pray that I can accept the cancer as God's gift."

"I know that my son or daughter won't return to faith in Jesus," another person told me, "but please pray that I can love them where they are."

After this happened over and over, I became perturbed. People were asking for prayer while doubting that their prayers could be effective. So, I changed the way I responded to their doubts. When the next person approached and told me they knew God wouldn't do what they requested, I stopped them.

"I see what you are saying, and why you may be skeptical," I told them, "but let's pray in faith." The rest of the afternoon, I said, "Let's ask that your illness is healed, that your family member returns to Jesus, that your relationship is healed."

Far too often we rationalize the miraculous elements out of our faith. This lack of faith is one reason we don't see many healings.

HEALING IN JESUS' NAME

James instructs believers to pray for healing and anoint people with oil, which is what Catholics do in the sacrament of the Anointing of the Sick.

We are to simply proclaim healing in Jesus' name, expect a

miracle, and then humbly accept the healing he gives. He always heals. Sometimes we just don't have the faith to see it.

How do we do this? You don't need oil. That is for priests and ordained ministers in the sacrament. All you need to do is reach out, lay hands on the person, if appropriate or possible, and proclaim healing. That is simple to do. We can also pray for healing for those in distant places, but we must believe it and proclaim it. It is up to Jesus to do the rest, then we humbly accept his work.

"Boldly expect a miracle of healing," I tell people, "and then humbly accept the healing God gives."

Expect a healing. See it. Visualize it. See it as happening right now, not just as something you hope for in the future.

And remember, Jesus always works a miracle. He always heals. He never ignores us when doing something he commanded us to do. The healing we receive might surprise us. It may be a physical healing. It may be a healing of thoughts and emotions. But God heals those with faith to ask and receive God's gifts.

OUR RESPONSE

You and I must respond to the healing God provides.

The paralytic man who was lowered into the room had to pick up his mat and walk.

Likewise, Jesus healed Peter's mother-in-law, and she quickly sprang back into action (Luke 4:37–39).

You and I must dare to act on the healing we receive from God, or we will stay stuck on the mats of our pain and sickness. We will grow accustomed to being sick. We might even subconsciously like the attention illness brings.

It can take great faith and courage to rise up and walk. We

must believe that we are healed, visualize it, and act upon it. We must rise.

I like this prayer written by the late Fr. Peter Rookey, another ordinary priest blessed with the extraordinary gift of healing:

Lord Jesus, I come before You just as I am. I am sorry for my sins, I repent of my sins, please forgive me. In Your Name I forgive all others for what they have done against me. I renounce Satan, the evil spirits and all their works. I give You my entire self, Lord Jesus, now and forever. I invite You into my life, Jesus. I accept You as my Lord, God, and Savior. Heal me, change me, strengthen me in body, soul and spirit. Come, Lord Jesus, cover me with Your Precious Blood, and fill me with Your Holy Spirit. I Love You, Lord Jesus. I Praise You, Jesus. I Thank You, Jesus. I shall follow You every day of my life. Amen Mary, my Mother, Queen of Peace. St. Peregrine, the Cancer Saint, all you Angels and Saints, please help me. Amen.[2]

Have you experienced a divine healing in your life?

Have you received this divine therapy that heals the body and soul?

Can you believe in healing by faith even when your current symptoms of sickness seem overwhelming?

Are you able to rise up from your mat of sickness and pain against all apparent odds?

To receive this gift of healing, you have to believe, seek God, and await his blessing.

CHAPTER 8

THE GIFT OF MIRACLES

WHEN THE SUPERNATURAL
INTERVENES IN THE NATURAL

You will receive power when the Holy Spirit
comes on you; and you will be my witnesses.
—ACTS 1:8

Miracles are everywhere, or so it seems. At least one thing is clear: there's a powerful hunger for the miraculous. Amazon.com offers more than one hundred thousand books dealing with miracles.

One of the bestsellers is a 1976 book called *A Course in Miracles* that became more popular after Marianne Williamson promoted it on *The Oprah Winfrey Show* in 1992. The book was supposedly dictated by Jesus, but it contradicts many key points of Christian teaching, and claims that our perceptions of everything in time and space are illusory.

Meanwhile, one Christian organization promises that people

who attend its crusades will witness "sevenfold miracles. . . . Such as neither humans nor angels have ever seen." These miracles, we are told, "will confirm the final march to the fall of America and the rise of the Antichrist."[1]

Christian miracle workers like Kathryn Kuhlman and Oral Roberts became famous in the twentieth century, but many people remain skeptical because there is a long history of con men and con women exploiting people's hopes by promoting bogus miracles and raking in money.

One of the most notorious hucksters was Peter Popoff, whose fake miracles were exposed in 1986 on Johnny Carson's *The Tonight Show* by James Randi, who made a career of exposing paranormal frauds. Randi's team took radio scanners to a Popoff "miracle" service and overheard assistants giving Popoff information about audience members through a hidden earpiece. Popoff closed down his ministry, but by the 1990s he was back in business and promoting "miracle spring water."

There is so much craziness and chicanery surrounding miracles that it's tempting to dismiss the whole subject. However, that would be a huge mistake, because God has used miracles for millennia. We shouldn't let hucksters prevent us from experiencing the Holy Spirit's powerful gift of miracles.

THE MISSION OF MIRACLES

Water in rivers turns to blood. Frogs and locusts cover the land. A mysterious plague kills all of Egypt's firstborn sons. The Red Sea parts, allowing Israelites to escape Egypt on dry land. Then, during their sojourn in the desert, manna is provided from heaven for their daily food.

Water flows from rocks. A donkey speaks. The walls of Jericho fall. One widow's son is raised, while another sees her cooking oil supernaturally multiplied. Daniel escapes from the lions' den.

The Old Testament is a book of miracles, and these supernatural manifestations shared a common purpose to demonstrate God's existence and power and to declare his divine will to people everywhere.

Jesus carried on this tradition. His life was bookended by miracles, starting with his virgin birth, and concluding with his resurrection from the dead and ascension to heaven. In between these bookends, some three dozen miracles were reported. One Catholic website (catholic-resources.org) breaks down Jesus' New Testament miracles into four categories:

- Exorcisms (casting out demons and unclean spirits)
- Healing miracles (healing physical illnesses and impairments)
- Restoration miracles (raising the dead; restoring to life)
- Nature miracles (feeding multitudes, calming storms)

Jesus commanded his disciples to carry on this miraculous ministry and promised them some help in doing so: "You will receive power when the Holy Spirit comes on you; and you will be my witnesses in Jerusalem, and in all Judea and Samaria, and to the ends of the earth" (Acts 1:8).

This passage was the basis for my song "You Will Receive Power."

You will receive power when the Holy Spirit falls upon you,
And you will be my witnesses to the ends of all the earth.
In the time after the suffering of the Lord

He showed us many ways he was still alive.
And he told us not to leave Jerusalem
Until we are bold clothed with the power on high.
You will receive power when the Holy Spirit falls upon you,
And you will be my witnesses to the ends of all the earth.

The apostles faithfully carried on this miraculous ministry, and after the day of Pentecost, the gift of miracles was granted to the church, as Paul recorded in four simple words: "to another miraculous powers" (1 Corinthians 12:10).

But Paul also made it crystal clear that this gift was not given to all believers: "Are all apostles? Are all prophets? Are all teachers? Do all work miracles?" (1 Corinthians 12:29).

A SUPERNATURALLY TURBO-CHARGED CHURCH

Church leaders made frequent use of God's miraculous power to demonstrate the truthfulness and divine inspiration of their teaching and to establish the church. This power was dynamic, as we see in the Greek word for both *power* and *miracle*: δύναμις (*dunamis* /*doo*·nam·is/). As previously mentioned, this is the root word for our word *dynamite*.

We see this power in action throughout the book of Acts:

- Peter heals a lame man at the temple (3:7–11).
- Ananias and Sapphira, who lie to the believers about their contributions to the church, are slain by the Lord (5:5–10).
- Angels and earthquakes open prison doors (5:19 and 16:26).

- Stephen (6:8) and Philip (8:6, 7, 13) work wonders and signs.
- Peter (9:39–42) and Paul (20:8–12) raise people from the dead.
- Paul heals a crippled man (14:8–18) and a woman possessed by an evil spirit (16:18).

Each of these miracles aided the growth of the church, but two others stand out.

In Acts 9, we see how the risen Christ appears to Saul, who is blinded and later healed (vv. 3–18). As we know, Paul—who once persecuted the church—would become its primary first-century evangelist.

And in Acts 10, Peter sees a miraculous vision and speaks with the risen Lord (vv. 9–22). After this miracle, Peter concludes that Christ's gospel should be proclaimed to all people, not only Jews.

The writer of Hebrews explained that these miracles were God's way of confirming and testifying to his power: "This salvation, which was first announced by the Lord, was confirmed to us by those who heard him. God also testified to it by signs, wonders and various miracles, and by gifts of the Holy Spirit distributed according to his will" (Hebrews 2:3–4).

Many miracles were attributed to Paul, a miracle worker with a powerful reputation: "God did extraordinary miracles through Paul, so that even handkerchiefs and aprons that had touched him were taken to the sick, and their illnesses were cured and the evil spirits left them" (Acts 19:11–12).

My Protestant friends make fun of the Catholic tradition of honoring the relics of saints, but the tradition of relics actually has its origin in passages like these. During the early days of the church, there were times when the use of objects that had simply touched Paul's body were said to carry the power of healing, so it is understandable that people would keep and honor such relics.

GOD'S DYNAMIC POWER AT WORK TODAY

If Jesus had wanted his first miracle to create a stunning, dramatic show, he could have done something big and loud in front of huge crowds. Instead, he started small, turning water into wine at a local wedding party (John 2:1–11).

Later in his ministry, there were plenty of dramatic miracles, including when he fed thousands of people with just a small amount of food. This famous miracle was necessitated by the success of Jesus' earlier miracles, as we see in John's gospel.

Jesus and his disciples crossed over to the far shore of the Sea of Galilee to briefly withdraw from the chaos of the crowds. But their efforts proved futile. "A great crowd of people followed him because they saw the signs he had performed by healing the sick" (John 6:1–3).

Our community, the Brothers and Sisters of Charity, may not play as important a role in God's grand plans as Peter and Paul did, but still, we have been privileged to witness his miracle-working power among us. On one occasion we experienced a miraculous multiplication of food at Our Lady of the Angels Mission, our community on the idyllic island of Ometepe in Nicaragua. Here's what happened.

A friend who often volunteered at our monastery was getting married, and we were hosting the wedding and the party afterward. We expected several hundred guests, and we planned accordingly, preparing enough food and beverages to serve 250 people. But little did we know that in Nicaragua, entire villages might show up for a wedding. Our event was to be no exception. More than 500 people arrived at our monastery.

We had ordered enough roasted pig for three hundred or more sandwiches, but it was clear once the crowd showed up and started eating that we would have nowhere near enough pork to go around. What could we do? We just kept on slicing ham for sandwiches, and somehow, as we did so, the size of the pig refused to diminish.

I was there and saw this miracle with my own eyes. No matter how many people came through the line for a first sandwich, or seconds, or even thirds, we never reached the end of that pork! All of us involved in this event agreed that we had witnessed a miracle that helped us minister and show hospitality to our Nicaraguan friends.

In another case, a team from our community in Arkansas was traveling across the United States to visit multiple parishes. My wife, Viola, is always an essential part of our itinerant ministry. As we were ministering in a small town in Illinois, she stepped on an uneven step, breaking her foot. All the team members who were with her could clearly hear that familiar but sickening sound of a bone snapping in two. She quickly prayed that through the intercession of Pope John Paul II, Jesus would heal her foot, and he did!

Because of my involvement in that day's program, I was unaware of her accident and healing until later that evening, when we all got back into the van we were traveling in.

"So, how did everything go today?" I asked.

"Jesus gave me a little miracle tonight," she said. "I broke my foot, but God healed it!"

Once our band of itinerants got back to Arkansas, Viola went to see her doctor. He confirmed that, indeed, the foot had been broken, yet had completely healed.

But I didn't require a doctor's confirmation. I have been with Viola for more than thirty years now, and I can testify that miracles are a regular part of her life, much more so than in my own life. As I considered why this might be the case, the answer was obvious. Viola has a deep and abiding faith in God and a childlike trust in his love and care for her. Such faith and trust create a more hospitable environment for the miraculous than my sometimes-skeptical approach.

SUN DANCING

While the miracle of the never-ending pig and Viola's healed foot helped our community minister more effectively, another miracle seemed designed simply to bring us joy.

In the late 1980s, two of our community members traveled to Medjugorje, a town in Bosnia and Herzegovina that became famous for apparitions (or appearances) of Jesus to believers. They had a positive experience there, but sensed God telling them they didn't need to go around the world to experience the presence of God.

They heard the words, *Medjugorje is at home*, which they understood as meaning *You can experience God's presence back at your community in Arkansas.* Then they heard the final words: *Go home.*

They returned to Arkansas, where a short time later they joined about eighty members and friends of our community in our annual Thanksgiving celebration. After our big meal, about half of our number went out for a hike in the valley that's home to our monastery so we could work off some of the turkey, potatoes, and gravy. We had walked about a mile up a big hill when we saw it.

The sun was dancing and spinning, as spots of gold began to appear on the monastery road before engulfing the entire valley. It was still early in the afternoon, so we weren't seeing the golden hue of a sunset. This was no normal phenomenon, as everything around us seemed to emanate a warm, golden glow. The lake exhibited a rainbow of colors of gold, red, and blues. Even our dog Bernie radiated a warm, golden glow!

We were caught up in the wonder of it all. We soon experienced outpourings of the Holy Spirit that caused our entire community to become enraptured in the Spirit. Two busloads of Christian pilgrims from Ukrainian Catholic parishes saw the sun dancing for themselves and experienced being slain in the Spirit once they stepped onto the ground in front of our chapel.

SUPERNATURAL OR NATURAL?

"It's a miracle!" says a woman who emerges without a scratch from a horrific accident that saw her Prius crushed to half its size between two semitrucks.

"It's a miracle!" say the weary new mom and dad, expressing their awe at the birth of their first child.

"It's a miracle!" says the athlete whose last-second goal or basket or touchdown wins the game for his team.

In one unusual case from May 2019, a driver in Viersen, Germany, was spared a speeding ticket when a snow-white dove flew in front of his windshield, blocking his face from police cameras, which meant he couldn't be identified and issued a ticket.

"It was no coincidence the Holy Spirit intervened," said the police, who hoped the speeder would slow down after this "hint from above."[2]

Are events like these really miracles, or are they natural phenomenon that occur on their own? This is the kind of seemingly simple theological question that is really quite profound and complicated. But let's make it as simple as we can.

God created everything that exists, and he sustains all of creation with his love and power to this very day. That means God is present and involved in the ordinary, mundane, and glorious events of daily life. The supernatural is present in the natural.

Miracles happen when God supernaturally intervenes in these natural events, but you and I don't always have the wisdom to tell the difference.

History has also shown us many cases of humans mistakenly claiming that natural events are supernatural because we simply didn't understand the science behind the events.

Take Halley's Comet, for example. For centuries, whenever people saw this alien visitor streak across the sky, they concluded it was heralding omens or supernatural events. It wasn't until 1705 that astronomer Edmond Halley calculated the comet's 1.7-billion-mile orbit and accurately predicted that it would return in 1758. Mystery solved. Halley's Comet is no longer seen as a supernatural omen but as an astronomical fact.

It can be difficult to distinguish natural events from supernatural breakthroughs, but whenever I'm not sure, I praise God anyway. When a child is born, or when a player returns a fourth-quarter kickoff a record 107 yards for a game-ending touchdown, or when a person emerges from a highway accident unscathed, I thank God and say hallelujah.

EXPECTING AND ACCEPTING
THE MIRACULOUS

How can we be open and available to God's miraculous power in our lives?

We must always expect a miracle. Then we must accept the

miracle that Jesus brings. If all we do is expect, we can easily cross over into the presumption of demanding gifts from God.

This requires both boldness and humility. We boldly approach the throne of grace (Hebrews 4:16), but we must have the humility of the tax collector, not the arrogance of the Pharisee (Luke 18:9–14).

We must have the boldness of faith necessary to see miracles. Boldly take Jesus at his word that he will answer prayers and work miracles in your life. But then have the humility to accept the miracle that he brings you.

Sometimes the miracle you receive is different from the miracle you prayed for, but if you don't have the boldness to pray for the first miracle, you may never receive the second miracle.

Jesus always works miracles! His answer is never no. As long as we ask in good faith, his answer is always yes! Our job is to ask and await his response. When we boldly expect and humbly accept, we will see miracles.

Miracles require a faith that may be difficult for many oh-so-rational people. Miracles require a faith that can see beyond what human eyes alone can see, beyond what the rational mind alone can understand.

We must dare to believe in supernatural intervention, even though those around us think we're silly or foolish. As Jesus said: "With man this is impossible, but with God all things are possible" (Matthew 19:26).

POWER FROM ON HIGH

Jesus promised to pass on a share of his miracle-working power to us, as we see at the end of Mark's gospel, where he gave his disciples a commission and a promise:

Go into all the world and preach the gospel to all creation. Whoever believes and is baptized will be saved, but whoever does not believe will be condemned. And these signs will accompany those who believe: In my name they will drive out demons; they will speak in new tongues; they will pick up snakes with their hands; and when they drink deadly poison, it will not hurt them at all; they will place their hands on sick people, and they will get well. (Mark 16:15–18)

What an exciting passage! Jesus is declaring that the Spirit's gifts will live on in his church. On the other hand, the passage has proven a bit too exciting for some interpreters. While Paul did in fact survive the bite of a deadly viper (Acts 28:1–6), many a snake-handling preacher has died from venomous snake bites. We should not tempt God (Matthew 4:7).

WARNINGS FOR THE
OVERLY EXCITED

For those who may get excited just thinking about the Spirit's gift of miracles, Jesus offers a stern warning about abusing this gift. Once again, the context is that a group of Pharisees is trying to trick Jesus:

Then some of the Pharisees and teachers of the law said to him, "Teacher, we want to see a sign from you."

He answered, "A wicked and adulterous generation asks for a sign!" (Matthew 12:38–39)

Later, Jesus issued an even stronger warning:

If anyone says to you, "Look, here is the Messiah!" or, "There he is!" do not believe it. For false messiahs and false prophets will appear and perform great signs and wonders to deceive, if possible, even the elect. See, I have told you ahead of time. (Matthew 24:23–25)

I alluded to this challenge in the song "The Cross Is Foolishness":

> Some look for miracles, some look for wisdom
> But we preach only Jesus crucified
> It seems absurdity, it seems so foolish
> But to us it is the wisdom of God

Miracles are real, but there will always be hucksters who try to sell us counterfeits. You need to be careful. Don't trust self-proclaimed miracle workers. Instead of letting these frauds make you skeptical about the real thing, follow the example of one believer who was frustrated by one TV preacher's attempt to manipulate and exploit God's gift of miracles.

Televangelists have long hawked prayer hankies, which I guess are the closest Protestants come to Catholics' religious relics. I've seen these shows myself. Toward the end, when it's time to ramp up the fundraising, some of these shows become marketing marvels, as preachers sell all manner of objects they claim are imbued with supernatural power.

One day a televangelist received so many requests for his prayer hankies that he ran out. A frantic ministry employee scrambled to find a solution: he took a photo of one of the prayer hankies and sent these photos to donors, instead of actual hankies.

One viewer came up with a brilliant response. She took a photo of a twenty-dollar bill and sent the photo to the ministry rather than her hard-earned cash.

You and I must have the faith to believe in miracles. We must be bold! Then we must humbly accept the miracle Jesus brings. Such miracles appear all around us every day, but it takes faith to see them. Then there are the breakthrough times when God does something that is undeniably supernatural and extraordinary.

God has entrusted his church with the gift of miracles. We must be cautious not to abuse this gift, which can bring harm to ourselves and to others.

CHAPTER 9

THE GIFT OF PROPHECY

EMPOWERED TO SHOW GOD'S TRUTH

*I wish that all the LORD's people were prophets and
that the LORD would put his Spirit on them!*
—NUMBERS 11:29

Moses gave the Israelites a choice combined with a warning.
If they obeyed God and followed his commandments, they
would experience many blessings: healthy children, bumper crops,
growing herds of livestock, and triumph over enemies.

But if they disobeyed God and rejected his commandments,
problems were sure to follow: newborns would be cursed, the land
would grow fallow, crops would fail, and enemies would prevail
over them (Deuteronomy 28–29; Leviticus 26).

Sadly, the Israelites would turn their backs on God. Moses'
prophecies would prove true. Disobedience paved the way for
destruction.

Some people equate prophecy with prediction, believing the prophets' primary work is foretelling the future. Foretelling is an important part of what God's prophets have done. For example, Jesus prophesied his own death and resurrection (Matthew 20:17–19). But future-telling is only one of the ways that God's prophets deliver divine messages.

Prophets speak for God about the past, present, and future. They warn sinners about the consequences of their disobedience. They comfort the persecuted with promises of their future redemption.

When people are blind and deaf to the reality of God, prophets make him real and visible. And when we still refuse to listen, they sometimes up the ante with drama and miracles.

God instructed the prophet Hosea to marry a prostitute so he could provide a living example of what Israel's unfaithfulness looked like (Hosea 1).

Even stranger, God instructed the prophet Jeremiah to bury his soiled undershorts in a crevice, leave them there for a good while, and then retrieve them. Now rotted and useless, the undershorts were used by Jeremiah as a powerful—and stinky—symbol of the people's disobedience. This prophet was a pioneering performance artist (Jeremiah 13:1–11).

A POWERFUL GIFT

From the beginning, prophecy has been one of God's most powerful tools for guiding people to him and his truth. Many books of the Bible are lengthy prophecies.

But Paul used only three words to announce this gift of the Spirit: "to another prophecy" (1 Corinthians 12:10).

Later, Paul revealed how important this gift is. "And God has placed in the church first of all apostles, second prophets, third teachers, then miracles, then gifts of healing, of helping, of guidance, and of different kinds of tongues" (1 Corinthians 12:28).

But with power and importance come responsibility and the risk of abuse. While I have received some prophecies that were real and shook my soul, I have also seen all manner of squirrelly things done in the name of prophecy.

For a while, a small group of people insisted that God wanted me to obtain blessed beeswax candles so I could burn them during a prophesied three days of darkness that were supposed to happen immediately. This was connected to St. Padre Pio's prophecy that said believers should keep the light of Christ shining during this time of great darkness.

I actually believe we *are* living in times of great darkness, but I never saw the prophesied blackout take place. And even though beeswax candles may be perfectly appropriate on altars during Mass, I don't believe we need to burn candles elsewhere as long as the electric lights still work.

That may seem like a silly example, but I've seen prophecy abused in serious and deeply destructive ways too. That's why we need to be on our guard. Over the centuries, the gift of prophecy has been exploited and twisted by devious people pursuing their own agendas, turning "divine guidance" into demonic deception. You and I need to make sure we know the real thing when we see it and can faithfully distinguish God's true prophecy from its false impostors.

We live in a time when many who are seeking God's truth desperately need his prophetic guidance. At the same time, many self-proclaimed prophets offer their unverified messages through religious TV shows, social media, and websites.

It's important that we understand this powerful gift. Let's start by looking at the key characteristics of both prophecy and prophets.

PROPHECY: SPEAKING FOR GOD

What makes prophecy prophetic? It's not delivery by a resounding voice, like Charlton Heston's booming Moses in the movie *The Ten Commandments*. It's not even religious-sounding language full of good Old English words like *thee*, *thou*, and *henceforth*.

The Greek word for *prophecy* is προφητεία (*propheteia / prof·ay·ti·ah/*), from προφήτης, meaning simply *"to speak before,"* or *"to speak from above,"* as an oracle or messenger of God.

Here we find our first characteristic of prophecy: it conveys God's truth. Today there are often multiple versions of "truth" competing for our trust. But God's truth is always truest, and prophets guide us to that supernatural knowledge. As *The Catholic Encyclopedia* says:

> The knowledge must be supernatural and infused by God because it concerns things beyond the natural power of created intelligence; and the knowledge must be manifested either by words or signs, because the gift of prophecy is given primarily for the good of others, and hence needs to be manifested.[1]

Prophets don't need to utter the words "Thus says the Lord." They might simply say they have a "word" from God, or they may simply speak as God's messenger. They may prophesy in the context of preaching and teaching. The important thing is that in both content and method, it is God's truth being shared, not our own opinions masquerading as God's.

Many prophets often describe the future, as we previously saw from the cases of Moses and Jesus. These prophets tell of coming events to prepare people for what is to come and to announce God's judgment on their sinful ways. But they might also speak for God powerfully about the past or the present, helping us understand God's perspectives on things that we don't understand. As *The Catholic Encyclopedia* explains:

> Understood in its [prophecy's] strict sense, it means the foreknowledge of future events, though it may sometimes apply to past events of which there is no memory, and to present hidden things which cannot be known by the natural light of reason.[2]

Another characteristic of prophecy is that prophets often challenge the status quo. When the Jewish people wanted to be ruled by a king like the other nations, the prophet Samuel acquiesced to their request, but he warned them about the unintended consequences of having a king, as opposed to the judges who had ruled them up to that point (1 Samuel 12:1–15).

Prophets sometimes have mountaintop experiences. Moses was on a mountain when God gave him the Ten Commandments. But prophetic words come in other ways as well. Sometimes God speaks in a "gentle whisper" (1 Kings 19:9–13), sometimes in visions (Ezekiel 1:1), and sometimes in dreams (Daniel 7:1).

Some people assume prophecy must always be lofty or mystical, but prophecy can help the church in practical and seemingly mundane matters. Cyprian of Carthage, a third-century bishop in North Africa, reported that prophecy was used in the appointment of leaders, for personal guidance, and for public direction to the local faith community. Cyprian also said prophetic visions comforted confessors—those who were about to die as martyrs for their faith.

PROPHETS: SERVANTS WHO ARE WILLING AND PREPARED

Prophets were given a prominent role in the early church. Some of the first apostles were also prophets, but the Spirit also blessed ordinary folks with this gift.

Because prophecy was a regular part of life of the church, various guidelines were developed for separating the good from the bad. Some of these guidelines were simple:

- Is the prophet a Christian who ascribes to orthodox theology?
- Is the prophet a disciplined believer whose life displays the fruits of God's Spirit?
- Is the prophet under the supervision of a bishop or pastor?

This is the picture that emerges: Prophets were men and women who loved God, were devoted to serving the church, gratefully received their prophetic gifts from God, and used these gifts to serve the community. Some of these prophets were even associated with prophetic schools that aided in their training. These prophetic schools were predecessors of later monastic communities.

The Didache (which was also called *The Teaching of the Twelve Apostles*) urged bishops to allow prophets to minister freely in their midst, but added these warnings. Prophets are to be rejected if they ask for money. They are to be rejected if they ask to be hosted for more than three days without ministering their gift. While we can't enforce these principles legalistically today, we should still watch out for moneygrubbers and couch surfers.

Mandate 11 of *The Shepherd of Hermas* (a book that many early church fathers considered part of the New Testament) offered additional simple tests: Godly prophets are humble, knowing that the gift is God's, not theirs. But false prophets are arrogant and proud. Godly prophets serve the church, while false prophets stay out on the fringe of local community.

The first-century bishop Ignatius of Antioch had an additional rule for prophets, particularly the itinerants who came and went: "Apart from the bishop let nothing be done." This wasn't some kind of early church power play. Ignatius was trying to protect Christ's flock at a time when many heretics claimed to speak for God.

In fact, two second-century schismatic groups claimed their prophecies were superior to the teaching of church bishops. We don't have space here to explore the heresies of the gnostic Valentinus and hyper-charismatic Montanus. But these ancient heretics and their followers were the equivalent of some of today's overheated Pentecostals or charismatics, who prioritize their own personal "prophecies" over the word of Scripture and the teaching of the church on core theological issues such as the Trinity.

These abuses of prophecy led to a gradual diminishment of prophecy in the church and greater reliance on clergy, bishops, and popes to play the prophetic role. Over the centuries, many papal encyclicals have proven to be prophetic.

THE END IS NEAR! (OR MAYBE NOT)

I came to faith in Christ through the Jesus movement of the 1960s and '70s, a period when end-time prophecies were popular. From

Hal Lindsey's bestselling book *The Late, Great Planet Earth* to the guy screaming on the street corner, I regularly heard the message "The end is near!"

This wasn't a new phenomenon. Apocalyptic prophets have been regular characters in the drama of the church from the beginning. They were particularly popular around the year 1000, and we saw millennial madness repeat itself just before the year 2000. Remember the Y2K crisis? Many Christians wrote bestselling books proclaiming that an obscure coding error would cripple the world's computers, wreaking havoc on businesses and government systems:

- Hal Lindsey's *Facing Millennial Midnight: The Y2K Crisis Confronting America and the World*
- Grant Jeffrey's *The Millennium Meltdown*
- Steve Farrar's *Spiritual Survival During the Y2K Crisis*
- Michael Hyatt wrote three separate Y2K books: *The Millennium Bug: How to Survive the Coming Chaos*, *The Y2K Personal Survival Guide*, and a novel, *Y2K: The Day the World Shut Down*.
- The Christian Coalition website predicted widespread "looting, robbery, (and) gang warfare," suggested President Bill Clinton might use the crisis to become America's "first dictator," and urged everyone to gather food, water, and bullets.

The world didn't end, exposing many false prophets who should be grateful we're not imposing the penalty Moses prescribed:

A prophet who presumes to speak in my name anything I have not commanded, or a prophet who speaks in the name of other gods, is to be put to death.

> You may say to yourselves, "How can we know when a message has not been spoken by the LORD?"
>
> If what a prophet proclaims in the name of the LORD does not take place or come true, that is a message the LORD has not spoken. That prophet has spoken presumptuously, so do not be alarmed. (Deuteronomy 18:20–22)

Sadly, today's false prophets often face no penalties when their falsehoods are exposed. They merely move on to their next "amazing prophecy." While it might seem harsh to propose the death penalty for false prophets, wouldn't it be nice if they donated the profits earned through their errors to Christian charities that could use the help?

"Watch out for false prophets," Jesus warned. "They come to you in sheep's clothing, but inwardly they are ferocious wolves. By their fruit you will recognize them" (Matthew 7:15–16).

Later with his disciples, he made a similar warning. "Watch out that no one deceives you. For many will come in my name. . . . False messiahs and false prophets will appear and perform great signs and wonders to deceive, if possible, even the elect" (Matthew 24:3–26).

PROPHECY IN ACTION

God's true prophets have guided God's people from the beginning of time. The prophecies in Jewish scripture focused largely on four areas: religious and ethical concerns; leadership; current crises and events; and future events.

In the book of Acts, we see prophecy up close and personal as a regular feature of the church. Paul fell into a trance and was given a prophetic warning to leave Jerusalem (Acts 22).

The prophet Agabus predicted a worldwide famine, and the disciples coordinated a relief fund to aid victims (Acts 11). Prophets guided the church to appoint Barnabas and Paul as evangelists to the Gentiles (Acts 13).

Prophecy continued throughout the Middle Ages, and was evident most powerfully in the life of St. Francis of Assisi. Jesus gave Francis a prophetic command: "Go repair my house, for as you can see it is falling into ruin." Francis took that as an order to rebuild a local church that had fallen down, but Christ had in mind a much bigger rebuilding project: reforming his global church.

In another case, when Francis sought the pope's blessing, he and the pope had simultaneous prophetic visions. Francis saw a great, tall tree reaching down to pick him up—a sign of the pope's future embrace. The pope saw a vision of a little beggar man struggling to keep a big church building from falling down—a sign of Francis's program of reform and renewal.

An early biography of Francis by his disciple Thomas of Celano described what would happen to Francis when the prophetic power absorbed him:

> He was then caught up about himself, and absorbed in a certain light; the capacity of his mind was enlarged and he can see clearly what was to come to pass. When this sweetness finally passed, along with the light, renewed in spirit, he seemed changed into another man.[3]

Francis delivered a series of prophecies that later came to pass, as Thomas of Celano described in his *Second Life of St. Francis of Assisi*:

- He foretold the defeat of the Crusaders at Damietta for trying to convert Muslims with force, rather than with love and truth.

- He predicted which individual brothers would leave the community, and could tell when people seeking entrance into the order were not led by the Spirit.
- He prophesied a famine that happened after his death.
- He predicted that his own little community of brothers and sisters would grow into a great community in the church that would spread across the world. Today, there are more than a million Franciscans around the world. Even my monastic vocation was largely inspired by Francis.

In the centuries after Francis, prophecy diminished somewhat. Protestant reformers Martin Luther and John Calvin taught that prophecy was limited primarily to the exposition of Scripture. This was a position adopted earlier by Origen and St. Thomas Aquinas.

Many Protestants remained skeptical about prophecy as unorthodox groups like the Mormons and the Shakers based their theology on new and controversial "revelations" from God. Much skepticism remained until the Pentecostal revival at Azusa in the early 1900s and the charismatic movement of the 1960s and '70s.

But prophecy remained a powerful gift. The Orthodox St. Seraphim of Sarov prophesied the coming Communist persecution in Russia and a following time of deliverance.

The children visited by Our Lady of Fatima were given prophecies relating to hell, World War I, and World War II.

And before he became Pope Benedict XVI, Fr. Joseph Ratzinger gave a powerful prophecy during a radio interview in 1969. He said that the church in the West would be stripped of its power and privilege, would lose most of its properties and prestige, and would begin meeting in small groups—perhaps in people's homes— where believers would rediscover authentic Christian experience. I have personally witnessed this prophecy being realized today.

I even heard that Corrie ten Boom, author of the Christian classic *The Hiding Place*, looked out an airplane window while flying over the Ozark Mountains of northwest Arkansas and prophesied that this area would become a place of refuge during an upcoming time of great persecution. The prophecy wasn't a factor in our choosing this area to establish the Little Portion Hermitage and Monastery, but if these hard times come, I hope we can stand strong and offer refuge.

SEEKING GOD'S PROPHETIC GIFT

Moses felt the same way I do. "I wish that all the LORD's people were prophets and that the LORD would put his Spirit on them!" (Numbers 11:29).

Likewise, Paul encouraged believers to let the prophetic gift do its work in our midst. "Do not quench the Spirit. Do not treat prophecies with contempt but test them all; hold on to what is good, reject every kind of evil" (1 Thessalonians 5:19–22).

I have sought this gift myself, and on occasion some people have called me a prophet, but I don't believe I am. Plus, as a general rule, it's unwise for prophets to declare themselves as such.

It is possible that some of my messages in my music and books and talks might be prophetic, but that may be because I have tried to adhere closely to God's Word in my work. I feel that I'm less a prophet and more a catalyst who brings together others to accomplish God's work while I disappear in the background, which is fine with me.

There was one time when the Lord gave me a biblical word regarding my life and ministry. The text was from the prophet Ezekiel: "To them you are nothing more than one who sings love songs with a beautiful voice and plays an instrument well, for they hear your words but do not put them into practice. When all this comes true—and it surely will—then they will know that a prophet has been among them" (Ezekiel 33:32–33).

Perhaps my ministry will have some lasting worth, at least in God's eyes and the eyes of a few of his people.

I encourage you to seek the Spirit's gift of prophecy, but let yourself be guided by Paul's detailed instructions for prophets in 1 Corinthians 14:1–33. Paul wants us to seek this gift ("Follow the way of love and eagerly desire gifts of the Spirit, especially prophecy"), but he wants the gift used to build up the church, not divide it ("God is not a God of disorder but of peace—as in all the congregations of the Lord's people").

I pray that prophets and prophecy can once again function in our lives and in our churches as they did in the early days of the faith, allowing both clergy and laity to have an important voice in our communal worship. Perhaps then Paul's vision will be realized:

> Consequently, you are no longer foreigners and strangers, but fellow citizens with God's people and also members of his household, built on the foundation of the apostles and prophets, with Christ Jesus himself as the chief cornerstone. In him the whole building is joined together and rises to become a holy temple in the Lord. And in him you too are being built together to become a dwelling in which God lives by his Spirit. (Ephesians 2:19–22)

CHAPTER 10

THE GIFT OF DISCERNING SPIRITS

GOD'S X-RAYS OF THE SPIRITUAL WORLD

Satan himself masquerades as an angel of light.
—2 CORINTHIANS 11:14

I never aggressively sought the Holy Spirit's gift of discerning spirits, but received the gift anyway. As the founder and spiritual father of the Brothers and Sisters of Charity Little Portion Hermitage and Monastery, the Spirit has granted me the ability to discern the spirits of men and women who are part of our community, as well as those who visit our monastery.

I can assure you that this gift wasn't given to me because of my superior holiness, but because discerning other people is an important part of my role in the community. And frankly, this gift can be a blessing and a curse. Often I wish I didn't know what God shows me.

When this gift is active, my meetings with men and women become more than one-to-one encounters as I am able to distinguish the presence of spiritual beings in our midst, at least for a few seconds, and sometimes for a minute or two.

SPIRITS: GOOD, BAD, AND UGLY

There are the cases when demonic spirits appear, sometimes in graphic detail, and I can see these fallen angels, or spirits, living in or hovering around the person across from me. This is never pleasant for me. (And so far, I have never yet seen a character dressed in red with horns and a pitchfork.)

I have not been given the gift of exorcism, so I don't try to expel evil spirits that have possessed people. This is serious business that's best left to those who are trained in spiritual warfare, such as a bishop with apostolic authority for this special ministry or a priest commissioned by a bishop. But when I do see these malevolent powers, I pray for the person's deliverance from demonic forces.

In other cases, I can perceive godly spirits in visual form. This is wonderful to experience. Angels are all around us at all times, but I seldom see them. When the Spirit gives me the gift of discernment, it's as though I'm suddenly looking through some kind of spiritual X-ray machine that sees through flesh and blood to the divine spirits animating a person's life and relationships. It is a joyful experience to witness these loving and holy spiritual beings present in and around an individual.

On other occasions, it's not divine or demonic spirits that I see, but rather the spirit of the particular person. Each one of us has a human spirit inside us. Our own human spirit is neutral and can choose between the Spirit of God, which inspires us toward goodness, or the temptations of demons.

It's a joyful experience to encounter a spirit that is childlike and joyfully open to God's love. In other cases, I can see a bruised and broken spirit—more like that of an abused child—that has been damaged by emotional or sexual abuse. Sometimes I see an old soul, twisted by the love of self or money, or simply worn down by the cares and worries of life. These human spirits appear dark, and are sometimes covered over by the weight of hurt, grief, or unconfessed sin.

All of this may sound rather fantastic, but my conversations with people play out in quite ordinary ways. Typically, as we talk these visions fade, but I use these flashes of spiritual discernment to help me minister to them, shape their growth and healing, and encourage them to address the challenges they face by loving God and conforming to his will.

I realize I may appear mad or medieval to people who believe that flesh and blood are all there is. But I think these people are missing out. There is more to life than the material. You and I have bodies and brains, but we are also spiritual beings, and we happen to be living in a spiritual world that is highly populated by all kinds of entities.

The Holy Spirit's gift of discernment is designed to help us see and navigate the spiritual realities that are often hidden within us and around us.

Some saints and theologians have argued that discernment may be the most important of the Spirit's gifts. That's because discernment plays an important role in many of the gifts, such as helping us distinguish the source of purported prophecies, words of knowledge, or miracles.

Let's see how God has used this powerful gift to illuminate our darkness and help us grow into his light.

DIFFERENT TYPES OF DISCERNMENT

The word *discernment* means different things to different people, and the word is used in a number of different ways in the New Testament.

GOOD VS. EVIL

Discernment is used to describe the ability Christians need to distinguish between good and evil. This form of discernment seems like a basic requirement of Christian living, but the author of Hebrews indicated that some believers lack this basic aptitude:

> We have much to say about this, but it is hard to make it clear to you because you no longer try to understand. In fact, though by this time you ought to be teachers, you need someone to teach you the elementary truths of God's word all over again. You need milk, not solid food! Anyone who lives on milk, being still an infant, is not acquainted with the teaching about righteousness. But solid food is for the mature, who by constant use have trained themselves to distinguish good from evil. (Hebrews 5:11–14)

ABUSING OF THE LORD'S SUPPER, OR EUCHARIST

The first-century Corinthian church faced a recurring problem: some members abused the liturgy of the Lord's Supper, turning it into a material meal rather than a spiritual celebration. Paul gave these people a stern warning:

So then, whoever eats the bread or drinks the cup of the Lord in an unworthy manner will be guilty of sinning against the body and blood of the Lord. Everyone ought to examine themselves before they eat of the bread and drink from the cup. For those who eat and drink without discerning the body of Christ eat and drink judgment on themselves. (1 Corinthians 11:27–29)

FINDING GOD'S WILL FOR ONESELF

One of the most common ways people talk about discernment today is when they are describing their own search to find God's will for their lives. Paul shows how an ongoing process of spiritual transformation will help us find God's perfect will for us:

Therefore, I urge you, brothers and sisters, in view of God's mercy, to offer your bodies as a living sacrifice, holy and pleasing to God—this is your true and proper worship. Do not conform to the pattern of this world, but be transformed by the renewing of your mind. Then you will be able to test and approve what God's will is—his good, pleasing and perfect will. (Romans 12:1–2)

We will explore more fully how you can discern God's will for your life at the end of this chapter, but for now let us turn to the type of spiritual discernment that will serve as the focus of this chapter.

GODLY AND EVIL SPIRITS

Paul introduced the Spirit's gift in his typical, brief manner: "to another distinguishing between spirits" (1 Corinthians 12:10). Here, the Greek word used for *discernment* is διάκρισης—*diakrisis*, which means to distinguish, discern, separate, judge, or decide. This refers to distinguishing between good and evil spirits and also to discerning a prophecy given in the community (1 Corinthians 14:29).

Numerous passages in the New Testament warn us that evil spirits are plentiful, and that they masquerade as godly spirits, requiring us to seek the Holy Spirit's protection and power. For example, Paul warned that evil spirits disguise themselves as good spirits, deceiving many within the church:

> I am afraid that just as Eve was deceived by the serpent's cunning, your minds may somehow be led astray from your sincere and pure devotion to Christ. For if someone comes to you and preaches a Jesus other than the Jesus we preached, or if you receive a different spirit from the Spirit you received, or a different gospel from the one you accepted, you put up with it easily enough. . . .
>
> Such people are false apostles, deceitful workers, masquerading as apostles of Christ. And no wonder, for Satan himself masquerades as an angel of light. It is not surprising, then, if his servants also masquerade as servants of righteousness. Their end will be what their actions deserve. (2 Corinthians 11:3–4, 13–15)

The apostle John issued a similar warning, but also provided a way to test the spirits by requiring them to acknowledge orthodox theology about Christ's divine nature:

> Dear friends, do not believe every spirit, but test the spirits to see whether they are from God, because many false prophets have gone out into the world. This is how you can recognize the

Spirit of God: Every spirit that acknowledges that Jesus Christ has come in the flesh is from God, but every spirit that does not acknowledge Jesus is not from God. This is the spirit of the antichrist, which you have heard is coming and even now is already in the world. (1 John 4:1–3)

You and I live in a spiritual world full of competing powers that seek our souls' embrace. Let's see how the spiritual gift of discerning spirits guided Jesus and empowered the church he founded.

JESUS' MINISTRY OF DISCERNMENT AND DELIVERANCE

Jesus was blessed with the gift of discernment, allowing him to look into people's souls and see their personal holiness, or lack thereof. Jesus often saw the inner thoughts of those around him, especially his adversaries (Matthew 9:4; Mark 2:8).

Sadly, Jesus saw that the rich young ruler loved his wealth too much to become a disciple (Mark 10:17–31).

Jesus also regularly discerned the hidden spiritual activity going on all around him, and in many cases the gift of discernment was paired with the gifts of healing and deliverance.

One day Jesus was teaching in a synagogue when a man stood up and cried out: "What do you want with us, Jesus of Nazareth? Have you come to destroy us? I know who you are—the Holy One of God!" Realizing that an unclean spirit was making the man speak that way, Jesus commanded the man to be quiet and commanded the spirit to come out of him (Mark 1:21–28).

Jesus often dealt with spirits this way, speaking directly to the spirits and bypassing the human beings who harbored them. In one case, he even commanded a spirit to reveal its name (Mark 5:1–20). Spirits are personal beings.

Though Jesus gave the gifts of discernment and deliverance to his disciples (Luke 9:1–2), they sometimes struggled to effectively exercise this gift, as we see in one passage from Mark.

One day Jesus saw a demon-possessed boy and asked his father to explain.

"Teacher, I brought you my son, who is possessed by a spirit that has robbed him of speech. Whenever it seizes him, it throws him to the ground. He foams at the mouth, gnashes his teeth and becomes rigid. I asked your disciples to drive out the spirit, but they could not."

But when the boy saw Jesus, the spirit made the boy convulse. Jesus rebuked the evil spirit and commanded him to come out of the boy, at which point the spirit "shrieked, convulsed him violently and came out."

When the disciples asked why they had not been able to drive the spirit out, Jesus said, "This kind can come out only by prayer" (Mark 9:14–29). Some later texts also add "and fasting."

The fact that Jesus' disciples struggled to cast out this evil spirit shows how difficult spiritual warfare can be, particularly when we fail to follow a holy, loving, and self-sacrificing way of life.

DISCERNMENT AND DELIVERANCE
IN THE CHURCH

The New Testament includes a shocking story about spiritual discernment that I think about every time I see people passing an offering plate at church.

In the very early history of the church, believers held their possessions in common, including their financial resources and income. But one couple tried to deceive their way out of this arrangement with deadly consequences. They sold a piece of property, gave some of the proceeds to the church, but hid some of the money for themselves, then lied about it. Their falsehood was easily discerned.

"You have not lied just to human beings but to God," Peter told the man, who fell down and died. Later, when the man's wife showed up and repeated the lie, she died too.

I suspect many people thank God they're not receiving that level of surveillance over their charitable giving!

Later, the apostle Paul was preaching in Cyprus when a sorcerer and false prophet tried to stop him (Acts 13:4–12). But Paul, who was filled with the Holy Spirit, looked at the man and delivered this verdict:

> "You are a child of the devil and an enemy of everything that is right! You are full of all kinds of deceit and trickery. Will you never stop perverting the right ways of the Lord? Now the hand of the Lord is against you. You are going to be blind for a time, not even able to see the light of the sun."
>
> Immediately mist and darkness came over him, and he groped about, seeking someone to lead him by the hand. (vv. 10–11)

Paul quickly transitioned from discernment of spirits, to verbal rebuke, to divine action. Not only was the sorcerer silenced, but a man observing the altercation was converted to faith in Christ.

In one unusual case, Paul and Silas discerned that spirits were enabling a female slave to predict the future, which she often did to make money for the man who owned her. Naturally, when Paul and Silas cast the spirit out of the woman, the man who had made a nice income from her predictions grew angry. He set the town against Paul and Silas, who were beaten and thrown into prison.

But this supernatural battle was not yet over. Later that night, an earthquake shook the prison. Paul and Silas could have walked out as free men, but they stayed to minister to the people in the prison, bringing many to faith in Christ (Acts 16).

Even stranger, one day some Jews who did not believe in Jesus tried to cast out demons in his name. One demon wasn't very impressed with their efforts to appropriate the Spirit's gift and lashed out at them verbally, before attacking them physically: "Jesus I know, and Paul I know about, but who are you?"

Then the man who had the evil spirit jumped on them and overpowered them all. He gave them such a beating that they ran out of the house naked and bleeding (Acts 19:13–20).

Evil spiritual forces have continued to attack God's work, even in the twenty-first century. Are we on the lookout for these malignant powers? And are we prepared to combat them?

LESSONS IN DISCERNMENT FROM THE DESERT FATHERS

For a crash course on spiritual discernment and duking it out with the Devil, I turn to the life and teachings of St. Antony and his fellow desert fathers and mothers.

According to some people, the desert fathers were a bunch of eccentric kooks. For example, Antony's biographer Athanasius said the saint "never bathed his body in water for cleanliness, nor even washed his feet, nor would he consent to put them in water at all without necessity."

Another father kept a stone in his mouth for three years so he could learn the discipline of silence. It apparently worked. He reportedly didn't speak for thirty years.

Like all of us, the fathers had their problems and excesses, but they knew a fair amount about the ways of the Devil and the tools God has given us to combat his efforts. They didn't see demons everywhere, as some of their harshest critics insist. Rather, they taught that demons are plentiful, are active, and move at Mach speed, enabling them to seem like they're everywhere.

The desert fathers and mothers can even be seen as ancient Christian psychologists, examining the ways evil spirits interact with our minds, and becoming experts in the battle for the soul that is primarily fought in the mind and our thoughts. They knew the battle for the soul begins in the mind and what we think matters.

Through their years of experience and study, the desert fathers broke down the millions of ways Satan tempts and attacks us into eight major vices that spring from our sinful thoughts. Thankfully, they also described the remedy for each vice. Let's look at their analysis.

VICE: GLUTTONY OR EATING GREEDILY

Even though gluttony may seem like a common, ordinary, sensual sin, it is important, for it can lead to the greater carnal sin of sexual immorality.

REMEDY: Gluttony is defeated with moderate fasting and by eating daily but not to satiety. And for the millions of Americans who are obese, perhaps a more realistic remedy for gluttony is eating moderately every day instead of overeating.

VICE: SEXUAL IMMORALITY

Not only is adultery a sin, but Jesus said looking at women and entertaining adulterous thoughts is sinful too. (Matthew 5:27–28)

REMEDY: Loving Jesus as our primary spouse defeats sexual sin.

VICE: AVARICE OR GREED

The constant hunger for more, newer, better. The need to possess or control things, situations, and people.

REMEDY: Avarice is overcome by living with other people in committed relationships in a family, or in a monastery in obedience to an abbot.

VICE: ANGER

That rage you feel when others hurt or threaten you.

REMEDY: Anger is overcome through forgiveness.

VICE: BITTERNESS

Bitterness comes when anger isn't healed, taking up residence in the dark corners of our heart.

REMEDY: Bitterness is overcome by developing an attitude of gratitude.

VICE: BOREDOM

Or lethargy, also known as listlessness, or acedia.

REMEDY: Boredom is overcome simply by doing something holy and constructive for God.

VICE: SELF-GLORIFICATION

The need to be noticed in little things is an important and often ignored vice that can lead to pride in major things.

REMEDY: Self-glorification is overcome by giving God all glory and praise for everything that exists, including all your blessings.

VICE: PRIDE

This vice is both the mother of the other vices and the end result of the other vices.

REMEDY: Pride is overcome by meditating on Jesus' suffering and death on the cross.

Among these eight vices, three seem the most destructive: gluttony, avarice, and self-glorification. These vices inevitably lead to other vices, as little sins lead to bigger offenses. Some of the vices lead to numerous other sins. For example, avarice can often lead to anger, bitterness, and boredom.

That's why we must know our spiritual enemies. That's the strategy the desert fathers and mothers embraced. Keeping your eyes open for these eight major vices can help you focus on the major battles you face.

DISCERNING GOD'S WILL FOR YOUR LIFE

I can't count the times people have asked me how to discern the will of God for their lives. I usually know the people who ask me, because they are members of our community who are seeking to discern their calling.

I don't know those of you reading this book quite so well, but based on my study of Scripture, especially the teachings of Jesus, I've concluded that we need to focus on these five tests:

1. TEACHING

As you seek to discern a life direction, or the will of God, find out as much as you can from sacred Scripture, apostolic tradition, and official church teaching. If your ideas don't line up with these proven sources, don't trust them.

2. COMMUNITY

Are you part of a monastic community or other faith community? Are you involved in ministry in the church, or at least in a Christian nonprofit or missions agency? If so, what do leaders and members of your community think?

3. GUIDANCE

Do you have a trusted spiritual director, spiritual father or mother, mentor, pastor, or counselor? What do they think?

4. INNER CIRCLE

Does your idea resonate with trusted spiritual friends who have known you over the long haul?

5. FRUIT

In Matthew 7 Jesus said we will know false prophets by their fruit. The same can be said about the fruit of his disciples. Does your proposed course of action produce the spiritual fruit Paul lists in Galatians 5: love, joy, peace, patience, kindness, mildness, generosity, chastity, and faith?

Use these five tests to get a broad-based perspective on your situation. If all five line up, you're standing on pretty solid ground.

EYES WIDE OPEN

Many false prophets have gone out into the world. Do you see them? Do you realize what they're trying to do?

Ask God to bless you with the Spirit's gift of discernment. I believe we need this gift today just as much as Paul and Peter did nearly two thousand years ago.

PART 3

CONCLUSION

CHAPTER 11

GOD'S OTHER
GOOD GIFTS

I t's another Christmas morning, and people around the world are joyfully shredding paper and opening presents. In many families, it's the big gifts in the shiny paper that go first, with smaller presents coming later.

Our response is similar when it comes to the Holy Spirit's gifts. Some—such as prophecy or speaking in tongues—get much of our attention, while other gifts generate less excitement.

In this chapter we will visit some of the Spirit's less celebrated gifts. Some of them are considered flashy or flamboyant, while others seem utterly mundane or natural. Some of these humbler gifts are listed alongside the other gifts in the New Testament. Others are only implied in Scripture, but have been experienced and attested to by Christian saints and mystics over the centuries.

Let's examine some of these lesser gifts to see what promise they hold.

ADMINISTRATION

While many people celebrate the supernatural nature of the Holy Spirit's gifts, one gift seems wholly natural: the gift of administration. But Paul included this practical gift alongside the more obviously supernatural gifts that often fascinate us more.

Paul listed the gift of administration in two of his letters. The gift gets one word in 1 Corinthians 12:27–28:

> Now you are the body of Christ and individually members of it. And God has appointed in the church first apostles, second prophets, third teachers, then miracles, then gifts of healing, helping, *administrating*, and various kinds of tongues. (esv, emphasis added)

The Greek word for this spiritual gift of administration is *kubernesis*, a unique term that refers to a shipmaster or captain who steers, rules, or governs. Variations of this word appear in Acts 27:11 and Revelation 18:17.

With this gift, the Holy Spirit empowers certain Christians to organize, direct, and implement plans to lead others in the various ministries of the church. This gift is closely related to the gift of leadership, but is more goal or task oriented, focusing on details and organization.

The gift of administration is often invisible, and the more effective this gift is, the less we are aware of it. Billy Graham was the star of his evangelistic crusades, preaching to more than two hundred million people at live events. But it took an army of noncelebrity organizers and volunteers to carry out the years-long planning and preparation process that made each of his events so successful.

I can understand if you think administration is boring or non-spiritual, but please don't write off this valuable gift too quickly. Have you ever noticed that church people can get quite upset when their favorite activities aren't well organized? We see such problems in the book of Acts, and they continue today (see Acts 6:1).

A godly administrator is not an overpowering control freak, but someone who lovingly serves, helping ministries work well for the benefit of all involved. But a bad administrator tries to control parishes and pastors, often becoming a proverbial log jam in the flow of the Spirit. A person who has the spiritual gift of administration facilitates the work of the Spirit rather than hinders it.

Clergy can also be administrators. In fact, more and more pastors are getting degrees in business and management so they can more effectively manage their churches and parishes.

Good training can be valuable, but pastoring and administration are two different gifts, and when pastors focus more on becoming CEOs than on serving as spiritual shepherds, churches can suffer. I have heard some people complain that church management conferences and conventions seem more like business meetings than spiritual conferences.

Administration may not sound exciting, but it is vitally important, as I have often seen for myself while ministering in hundreds of Catholic, Anglican, Protestant, and evangelical churches around the world.

Some congregations or events are well run (they're often successful), while some churches leave details to take care of themselves (they are often well meaning but less successful). When I am involved in my itinerant ministry, I can usually tell a well-managed parish when I walk onto the parish grounds. I can also tell many sad stories of administrators who bungled the

Spirit-filled directives of a pastor or congregation, killing good plans through bad management and execution.

I urge you to seek God and request this special gift, which won't get you as much attention as the gift of prophecy or tongues, but may actually have a greater impact on the harmony and effectiveness of Christ's work.

BEING SLAIN—OR RESTING— IN THE SPIRIT

Judas had betrayed Jesus, and now the Roman soldiers were seeking him out. But when he announced himself to them, something unusual happened:

> "I am he," Jesus said. (And Judas the traitor was standing there with them.) When Jesus said, "I am he," they drew back and fell to the ground. (John 18:5–6)

Similar experiences have happened throughout church history, most of them more positive than the encounter with the soldiers. In one case, St. Francis's friars were praying together when they looked up and saw Jesus standing in their midst. The book *The Little Flowers of St. Francis* reports that the brothers fell asleep as dead men. Today we would call that resting in the Spirit.

I have experienced this gift myself, starting more than thirty years ago during an outpouring of the Holy Spirit at one of our community-wide gatherings at the Alverna Center in Indianapolis, Indiana. The peace of Jesus overcame me, and I simply could not stand. I fell down in the presence of the Lord.

It was extremely calm, not violent at all. I was fully conscious of what was going on around me, but I could not speak. I felt that I could have come out of this experience by an act of my own will, but it was so peaceful that I simply didn't want to. I stayed resting in the Spirit for a very long time. Since that time, I have had this experience several other times.

Theologians have argued over whether this is actually a gift of the Spirit. Some say such occasions are caused by the Devil, not Christ. John Wesley, the Methodist founder who often saw people fall down during his preaching, considered this a natural human response to the supernatural presence of the Holy Spirit during conversion.

The arguments continue, as do testimonies about experiencing this unique gift. Even if you are not thrown to the ground by God's power, you can practice kneeling or prostrating yourself in prayer as a way of forsaking your pride and power and submitting to God's sovereign power. You simply stop standing by your own power and rest in the arms of God.

Paul wrote that God has exalted Christ and that "every knee should bow" at his name (Philippians 2:9–11). There's something beautiful when people humbly kneel and prostrate themselves before God. We shouldn't need the Spirit's intercession to embrace these physical gestures of our total dependence on God.

TEARS

"Blessed are those who mourn," said Jesus, "for they will be comforted" (Matthew 5:4).

"Rejoice with those who rejoice," wrote Paul, "mourn with those who mourn" (Romans 12:15).

Does the Spirit give certain people a supernatural gift of tears? Through the centuries, many saints and mystics have said yes. St. Symeon the New Theologian, who lived in the tenth century, described the gift of tears as follows:

> He who is interiorly illuminated by the Holy Spirit cannot bear the sight [the sudden streak of lightning flashes and the resplendence of the Spirit within] . . . he becomes like one who's entrails are touched by fire, devoured by the flame, unable to endure the burning; he is beside himself and cannot contain himself, but sheds abundant tears which refresh him, and stir up the flame of his desire; then his tears become more abundant and, purified by this flood, he shines with much brilliancy. Then, wholly inflamed, he becomes like the light.[1]

A few years back, I experienced this gift during a serious bout with illness that landed me in the hospital. I was in so much pain that it was difficult to pray with my mind, so all I could do was pray in tongues and weep.

One day during prayer, I sensed that my guardian angel and an angelic coworker lifted me up—one angel under each arm—and took me to a place where I could see Paradise in the near distance. Then the angels simply turned me around and brought me back.

I was simultaneously filled with humility, repentance, and an overwhelming joy. That's when I experienced tears in a new way. Since that experience, it has been easier for me to respond to God's love and grace with gentle tears, especially when receiving Jesus in the Eucharist.

RAPTURE AND ECSTASY

Paul adopted an unusual style in describing one of his spiritual experiences, using the third person:

> I know a man in Christ who fourteen years ago was caught up to the third heaven. Whether it was in the body or out of the body I do not know—God knows. And I know that this man—whether in the body or apart from the body I do not know, but God knows—was caught up to paradise and heard inexpressible things, things that no one is permitted to tell. (2 Corinthians 12:2–4)

Paul was caught up, or as other translations put it: raptured, captured, snatched, or pulled. He experienced ecstasy and was later given a "thorn in [his] flesh" (v. 7) to prevent him from being boastful about this experience. And as I described earlier, I have also experienced being "caught up" and taken to heaven, and experienced similar ecstasy.

Think of rapture and ecstasy as *falling up* to distinguish this experience from the *falling down* that happens when one is slain in the Spirit, or during prostration or kneeling. Fr. Adolphe Tanquerey devoted a whole section of his 1930 book *The Spiritual Life* to this phenomenon, which has happened throughout church history. The lives of St. Francis and his disciples are full of such reports.

In one case, Brother John of Alverna was celebrating the liturgy when he was overcome by the presence of Christ in the bread and the wine. He went into rapture and became oblivious to what was going on around him. He seemed suddenly stuck, with his hands up in the air and his body completely stiff and straight. Mass could not be completed right away, so the brothers simply lifted John up and gently leaned him against a nearby wall until he loosened up again.

Brother Giles of Assisi would reportedly go into rapture and ecstasy whenever he heard or even thought about the name of Jesus. This could be inconvenient! In one case, Giles met with the pope, and the pope did something popes often do: said the name of Jesus. Giles went into rapture and became oblivious to his surroundings. That ended their meeting, and Giles returned to his hermit's cave.

I have also heard reports that St. John Paul II experienced something similar while officiating at a major public event with many thousands of people in attendance. During one Eucharistic prayer at a huge public Mass, he went into rapture and ecstasy, requiring his attending priests to pull on the sleeve of his vestments and say something like: "Holy Father, there are a million people waiting for you, and we need to get on with it!"

I have experienced rapture when praying alone by myself in my hermit's cell, or with Viola, or even during Mass. In one case, I felt as if I was falling upward, certain I was levitating. I also experienced an intense heat in my hands, which made me think I was experiencing some kind of stigmata. But then I came out of it, and I was sitting right there on the ground—not ascending into the air—and had no wounds at all.

LAUGHTER

Reporters called the revival that broke out in 1994 the "Toronto Blessing," and they described one unusual manifestation that characterized the revival at the Toronto Airport Vineyard Church: holy laughter.

The book of Ecclesiastes said there is a time for everything: "a time to weep and a time to laugh" (Ecclesiastes 3:4). But does spiritual revival provoke outbursts of joy that result in holy laughter?

I have not experienced this gift, but I have enjoyed almost uncontrollable laughter with friends or when singing with others in the studio. I take a cautious approach with this manifestation, which is difficult to find in Scripture, has been ridiculed and even condemned by many, and has had little impact on the early church, the saints, or even Pentecostal and charismatic traditions.

We know that "laughter is good for the soul," but it is not always welcome in Scripture. Both Abraham and Sarah laughed in surprise when they were told that she was to have a child long after her childbearing years had passed. Their skeptical laughter was not a good thing (Genesis 17:17; 18:10–15).

Sirach agrees, saying profoundly that the fool lifts his head back in laughter, but the wise smiles gently, at most (Sirach 21:20).

There have also been reports of revivals where laughter appeared alongside alleged manifestations such as roaring like an animal. But is this behavior consistent with Paul's teaching that in church "everything should be done in a fitting and orderly way" (1 Corinthians 14:40)?

I'm not so sure. Be careful with this one.

STIGMATA

As he closed his letter to the believers in Galatia, Paul included this curious comment:

> From now on, let no one cause me trouble, for I bear on my body the marks of Jesus. (Galatians 6:17)

Most Bible scholars say this refers to the physical punishments and abuse he suffered as he was persecuted for spreading the gospel. But some scholars see a possible biblical prefiguring of stigmata, which are understood as crucifixion-type wounds on the hands and feet that have been experienced by St. Francis and other saints and mystics.

According to Francis's biographers, he first reported bearing Christ's wounds in his heart, and these wounds only manifested on his body later. Some say the stigmata appeared after Francis was rejected by the very community that he founded. Others say the stigmata appeared later in his life when he suffered many physical illnesses.

Still others say the stigmata were the culmination of Francis's lifelong experience of sorrow and joy. The sorrow was for sins, and the joy was for the glory that God nonetheless allowed him to experience in and through the forgiveness offered in Jesus Christ. When sorrow and joy were combined, these paradoxical feelings reportedly overwhelmed his mind and emotions.

Since Francis's time there have been many stigmatists reported in Western Christianity, the most famous being St. Padre Pio, the Italian mystic who died in 1968. I personally met one stigmatist. She was a holy, humble, and very ordinary person who was traveling with her bishop from Italy. She sought to meet with my bishop and then with me.

When the three of us met, and our conversation turned to our love for Jesus, she began to bleed from wounds in her head. She then expressed embarrassment about the bleeding but said this is what happened to her on occasion. Because of the woman's humble spirit, and the authenticity of the bleeding, I came away from this conversation convinced I had seen a manifestation of God's spiritual power.

I see many people pray for the gifts of prophecy and tongues, but few seek the gift of stigmata. Perhaps that's just as well. Padre Pio never sought this gift, but received it anyway, and said the wounds were very painful and embarrassing.

We are called to mystically bear the stigmata of Christ in our hearts and our souls as we meditate on him who was pierced for our offenses. This stigma of the heart is the kind of manifestation we should desire to receive.

EXPERIENCING GOD'S MANY GOOD GIFTS

In writing about the gifts of the Spirit, I have focused on the major gifts that are described in these five key New Testament passages:

- 1 Corinthians 12:8–10
- 1 Corinthians 12:28–30
- Romans 12:6–8
- Ephesians 4:11
- 1 Peter 4:11

I urge you to carefully study these passages and prayerfully seek God's will for your life. He has many good and powerful gifts to give his children if we are open and willing to receive them and committed to using them for his service.

God has given his children many good gifts, too many to cover in this book. My general approach when considering these other gifts is to find out if they are focused on Jesus and if they promote the good of the church. If they pass these two tests, I gratefully receive them as God's good gifts.

CHAPTER 12

LOVE IS THE
BETTER WAY

Without love, I am nothing.

Singer and songwriter Joni Mitchell was famous for her poetic lyrics, but when creating her song "Love," she borrowed from one of the most beautiful pieces of poetry in the Bible, the famous "love" chapter in Paul's first letter to the Corinthians.

Whereas the apostle concluded his passage about love with, "And now these three remain: faith, hope and love. But the greatest of these is love" (1 Corinthians 13:13), I have to admit, I'm a bit fond of how Mitchell poetically described the greatest of these "fractions," as she put it, of faith, hope, and love: *Love's the greatest beauty.*

PAUL'S POEM OF LOVE

There's a remarkable shift in tone from Paul's down-to-business language in 1 Corinthians 12 to his poetic tone in chapter 13.

Let's take a look at what Paul is saying in his opening three stanzas, stopping along the way to savor each powerful line:

> If I speak in the tongues of men or of angels, but do not have love, I am only a resounding gong or a clanging cymbal. If I have the gift of prophecy and can fathom all mysteries and all knowledge, and if I have a faith that can move mountains, but do not have love, I am nothing. If I give all I possess to the poor and give over my body to hardship that I may boast, but do not have love, I gain nothing.

LOVE DEFINED

Next, Paul describes in 1 Corinthians 13 what love is and what it isn't. Instead of offering heavy, academic prose, he offers simple sentences consisting of brief phrases packed full of concrete images:

> Love is patient, love is kind. It does not envy, it does not boast, it is not proud. It does not dishonor others, it is not self-seeking, it is not easily angered, it keeps no record of wrongs. Love does not delight in evil but rejoices with the truth. It always protects, always trusts, always hopes, always perseveres. Love never fails.

LOVE IS MORE IMPORTANT THAN GIFTS

Now, Paul returns to his discussion of spiritual gifts from above. It's here that the apostle gives us the wise warning we need when we're tempted to abuse these gifts for our own pleasure or power or gain:

But where there are prophecies, they will cease; where there are tongues, they will be stilled; where there is knowledge, it will pass away. For we know in part and we prophesy in part, but when completeness comes, what is in part disappears.

TO KNOW GOD IS TO LOVE GOD

Finally, Paul shifts once more, moving beyond a discussion of the spiritual gifts to reflections on the true nature of life and faith:

When I was a child, I talked like a child, I thought like a child, I reasoned like a child. When I became a man, I put the ways of childhood behind me. For now we see only a reflection as in a mirror; then we shall see face to face. Now I know in part; then I shall know fully, even as I am fully known. And now these three remain: faith, hope and love. But the greatest of these is love.

LOVE AS A WAY OF LIFE

As Paul described it, love is a way, not a gift. It's a way of life that underlies and permeates the gifts. And absent this way of love, the gifts are empty and shallow at best.

The Bible uses different words to describe different kinds of love, but the kind of love Paul described to the Corinthians is similar to the self-giving, self-emptying form exemplified by Jesus. Paul described Jesus' love in a passage from his letter to the church in Philippi. Read and reflect on this passage as you seek to know what love is:

In your relationships with one another, have the same mindset as
Christ Jesus:

> Who, being in very nature God,
>> did not consider equality with God something to be used
>> to his own advantage;
> rather, he made himself nothing
>> by taking the very nature of a servant,
>> being made in human likeness.
> And being found in appearance as a man,
> he humbled himself
>> by becoming obedient to death—
>> even death on a cross!
>> (Philippians 2:5–8)

You and I can only know this kind of love through death to self.
We must let the old self die, alongside Jesus on the cross, and let a
new person be born in its place. As long as I am a typical, ego-driven
man, I will never know this love, regardless of how many religious
rules and words I know. We must empty ourselves of false love and
self-love before we can experience the real thing: divine love. Love
that empties itself for the sake of another brings new life in Christ.

That's why scholastic Christian fathers often defined love as
the mutual outflow of oneself for the sake of another.

Traditionally, churches have celebrated monogamous, hetero-
sexual marriage as sacramental because it physically represents the
mutual self-giving and procreative love existing between Christ
and his bride, the church. If the man and woman are blessed
to have a child together, their family unit symbolizes the love
within the Triune God. As two pour themselves out completely
for the benefit of each other, a new life is created in the process.

Such procreation is a sign of the relationship between Jesus and his church. As he joins with us, together we create new life, new Christians, or "little Christs."

LOVE IS THE ONLY WAY

St. John of the Cross taught his followers that they should be prepared to answer this question after they died: How well have you loved?

You don't need to wait until death to ask that question. It's better if we ask it every day.

How well have you poured yourself out for God and for others?

Paul knew some people become giddy about spiritual gifts, but he told us it's not about the gifts. It's about the love.

All our theology, liturgy, sacraments, and common life exist only for one purpose: love. All these things exist so we might know love—through our personal union with Jesus Christ and through our shared life in communion with our brothers and sisters.

Love is all that matters.

GIVING IT ALL AWAY

The word Paul used for "emptied" is κενόω (*kenoo* /ken·o·o/), which means to make void, or vain, or of no reputation (Philippians 2:7).

That's the kind of love God calls us to. A love that is the complete emptying of ourselves for God and for others.

But lo and behold, it's when we give it all away that we are made full. Only when we die by giving ourselves in love do we come alive again and discover who we really are in Christ. This is just one of many paradoxes we experience in our Christian lives. "Whoever finds their life will lose it, and whoever loses their life for my sake will find it" (Matthew 10:39).

I wrote about this kind of love in the song "Philippians Canticle":

And if there be therefore any consolation
And if there be therefore any comfort in his love
And if there be therefore any fellowship in spirit
If any tender mercies and compassion
We will fulfill his joy
And we will be like-minded
We will fulfill his joy
We can dwell in one accord
And nothing will be done
Through striving or vainglory
We will esteem all others better than ourselves
This is the mind of Jesus
This is the mind of Our Lord
And if we follow him
Then we must be like-minded
In all humility
We will offer up our love

YOUR CONTINUING JOURNEY WITH GOD'S GIFTS

Thank you for joining me in this study of the gifts of the Holy Spirit, which is actually only a partial study, at best, of this important subject.

We are now coming to the end of this book, but I hope this is not the end of your journey with the gifts of the Spirit.

How can you act on what you have learned thus far? Here are some practical suggestions.

SEEK AND ASK FOR THE SPIRIT

Jesus taught his disciples how to pray, and right after he gave them the model prayer we call the Lord's Prayer, he promised that God the Father would send the Holy Spirit to those who asked him for it (Luke 11:13).

Paul's answer is equally simple: "Follow the way of love and eagerly desire gifts of the Spirit, especially prophecy" (1 Corinthians 14:1).

Ask God for the Spirit's gifts. Then dare to receive what God gives you. You might not receive what you are seeking immediately or all at once. But the Spirit will bless you if you hold nothing back.

LISTEN

I believe that if you and I listened and looked more deeply for God's presence and activity in our midst, we would experience his manifold and countless gifts every day of the year.

We must learn to quiet our minds and hearts so we can hear the still, small voice of God's Spirit.

ACT

Dare to do something. If you want to pray in tongues, open your mouth and make some sounds.

Other gifts may come in time. For example, if you seek the Spirit's gift of words of wisdom or knowledge to share with others, practice deep listening—both to them and to the Spirit in your midst. If the Spirit gives you a word, share it. If not, remain silent.

You won't receive every gift. God's in charge of distribution. But if you are open and humble, you will receive the gifting of the Spirit God wills for you.

Learn from Others

One way to grow in your walk with the Spirit is by being with people and faith communities that seek the Spirit's presence and gifting. Some established charismatic and Pentecostal churches offer classes in the gifts of the Spirit. You can also go to charismatic prayer meetings or Masses.

Join in with others in praising God, thanking him, worshipping him, and singing songs to him from your heart. Allow yourself to be prayed over by wise and experienced leaders.

Pray for Renewal

The Spirit's gifts are special channels through which God chooses to empower his children, but let's not get too obsessed about the gifts themselves. The gifts are only means and manifestations of the Spirit's power. Our goal should be to live in the Spirit.

I have seen how Africa and Asia are experiencing Spirit-filled revivals. Their churches are growing by leaps and bounds. In the West, many of our churches are dying. But we can be revived if we will open ourselves to the power of the Holy Spirit and operate in the gifts of the Spirit.

We desperately need a Spirit revival in the church today. We need the Spirit to fill us. We need to seek and use the Spirit's manifold and countless gifts every day of the year.

Pray that God will renew us and fill us with his Spirit.

SERVE OTHERS, NOT YOURSELF

In the end, it is love that matters. All the gifts begin and end in the love of God.

If you love God, and if you seek his calling for how you can serve his children, ask him to empower you with the Holy Spirit's gifts.

Go with his blessing as you proclaim Jesus and build up his church.

ACKNOWLEDGMENTS

John Michael Talbot thanks:

The Catholic Charismatic community in Indianapolis, Indiana, who were the first to show me that Catholics were highly charismatic, yet rooted in ancient Christian history.

Viola Talbot, who taught me how to really be fully alive in the Spirit in daily life.

Fr. Ralph Tichenor SJ, Dominic Berardino, and all at Southern California Renewal Communities, who opened the way of the Catholic Charismatic Renewal to me.

The Brothers and Sisters of Charity, who supported me in my integrated monastic life in the Spirit.

The many, many leaders, too numerous to name, who taught me about the gifts of the Spirit during my four decades of ministry.

Sr. Mary Kiara Elder of the Brothers and Sisters of Charity for her help citing quoted sources.

––––––

Steve Rabey thanks:

Members of the One Way House, a Jesus movement fellowship

in Springfield, Ohio, and other charismatic Christians from Protestant, Catholic, Anglican, and Orthodox traditions, who helped me experience the reality of the Holy Spirit in my life.

Wise professors at Denver Seminary, including Craig Blomberg (New Testament), and Timothy Weber and Bruce Shelley (church history).

Lois Mowday Rabey, who helped me write this book.

NOTES

CHAPTER 1: ALIVE IN GOD'S SPIRIT

1. William A. Jurgens, *The Faith of the Early Fathers*, vol. 2 (Collegeville, MN: Liturgical Press, 1970).

2. Jeff Oliver, *Pentecost to the Present, Book 1: Early Prophetic and Spiritual Gifts Movements* (Newberry, FL: Bridge-Logos, 2017), Kindle, p. 249.

3. William A. Jurgens, *The Faith of the Early Fathers*, vol. 1 (Collegeville, MN: Liturgical Press, 1970).

CHAPTER 2: THE SPIRIT AND THE GIFTS

1. Bernard M. Peebles, ed., *The Works of Saint Cyril of Jerusalem* (Washington, DC: Catholic University of America Press, 2000).

2. Alexander Roberts and James Donaldson, eds. *The Ante-Nicene Fathers / The Apostolic Fathers, Justin Martyr, Irenaeus* (Peabody, MA: Hendrickson Publishers, 2004).

3. Roberts and Donaldson, eds. *The Ante-Nicene Fathers.*

4. Roberts and Donaldson, eds. *The Ante-Nicene Fathers.*

5. Origen et al., *Against Celsus (Contra Celsum): The Complete English Translation from the Fourth Volume of the Ante-Nicene Fathers* (Ex Fontibus, 2013).

6. Saint Augustine et al., *A Select Library of the Nicene and Post-Nicene Fathers of the Christian Church. Vol. II St. Augustin's City of God*

and Christian Doctrine, ed. Philip Schaff, L.L.D. (Buffalo, NY: The Christian Literature Co., 1887).

7. John Calvin et al., *Calvin's New Testament Commentaries* (Grand Rapids, MI: Wm. B. Eerdmans, 1994).

8. Athanasius and John Henry Newman. *Select Treatises of S. Athanasius, Archbishop of Alexandria, in Controversy with the Arians* (London: John Henry Parker, 1842).

CHAPTER 3: THE GIFTS OF TONGUES AND INTERPRETATION

1. Jordan Daniel May, *Global Witnesses to Pentecost: The Testimony of "Other Tongues"* (Cleveland, TN: Cherohala Press, 2013).

2. May, *Global Witnesses to Pentecost: The Testimony of "Other Tongues."*

3. Gerald Lewis Bray and Thomas C. Oden, eds., *Ancient Christian Commentary on Scripture 1–2 Corinthians*, vol. VII (Westmont, IL: InterVarsity Press, 1999).

4. Saint Augustine et al., *A Select Library of the Nicene and Post-Nicene Fathers of the Christian Church*, vol. VIII (Whitefish, MT: Kessinger Publishing, 2004).

CHAPTER 4: THE GIFT OF WISDOM

1. Bernard Marr, "How Much Data Do We Create Every Day? The Mind-Blowing Stats Everyone Should Read," *Forbes*, September 5, 2019, www.forbes.com/sites/bernardmarr/2018/05/21/how-much-data-do-we-create-every-day-the-mind-blowing-stats-everyone-should-read/#211ff81260ba.

2. Thomas Aquinas, *Summa Theologica* (Sumptibus P. Lethielleux, Bibliopolae Editoris, 1925).

CHAPTER 5: THE GIFT OF KNOWLEDGE

1. Elise Harris, "The Modern—and Little Known—Miracles of Padre Pio," Catholic News Agency, accessed December 13, 2019, https://www.catholicnewsagency.com/news/the-modern-and-little-known-miracles-of-padre-pio-90983.

2. Saint Augustine and Philip Scaff et al., *St. Augustin's City of God and Christian Doctrine* (Grand Rapids, MI: Wm. B. Eerdmans, 1973).

3. Teresa of Ávila, *The Life of Saint Teresa of Ávila by Herself* (London: Penguin Books; New York: Viking Penguin, 1957).

4. Saint Teresa and Edgar Allison Peers, *Interior Castle* (Danvers, MA: Image Books, 1961).

5. Thomas Merton, *The Seven Storey Mountain* (SPCK, 2015).

CHAPTER 6: THE GIFT OF FAITH

1. Philip Schaff and Henry Wace, *A Select Library of Nicene and Post-Nicene Fathers of the Christian Church*, vol. VII (Peabody, MA: Hendrickson Publishers, 2004).

2. "Joint Declaration on the Doctrine of Justification," Vatican, last modified 1999, http://www.vatican.va/roman_curia/pontifical _councils/chrstuni/documents/rc_pc_chrstuni_doc_31101999 _cath-luth-joint-declaration_en.html.

CHAPTER 7: THE GIFT OF HEALING

1. Roy Porter, *The Greatest Benefit to Mankind: A Medical History of Humanity* (New York: W. W. Norton, 1997), 88.

2. Father Peter Rookey, "Miracle Prayer," March 16, 2012, http:// www.prayerflowers.com/prayergarden/index.php?topic=576.0.

CHAPTER 8: THE GIFT OF MIRACLES

1. https://www.sevenfoldmiraclecrusades.com/.

2. "Dove Saves Driver Who Should Have Gotten a Speeding Ticket." KFOR.com. Last modified May 29, 2019, https://kfor .com/2019/05/29/driver-who-shouldve-gotten-a-ticket-was-saved -by-the-holy-spirit/.

CHAPTER 9: THE GIFT OF PROPHECY

1. Robert C. Broderick, *The Catholic Encyclopedia* (Nashville: Thomas Nelson, 1987).

2. Broderick, *The Catholic Encyclopedia.*
3. Thomas Celano, *The Life of St. Francis of Assisi and The Treatise of Miracles,* trans. Catherine Bolton (Assisi, Italy: Editrice Minerva, 1997).

CHAPTER 11: GOD'S OTHER GOOD GIFTS

1. G. E. H. Palmer et al., *The Philokalia: Vol. 4, the Complete Text* (Faber, 1998).

ABOUT THE AUTHORS

John Michael Talbot is the founder and spiritual father of the Catholic-based community the Brothers and Sisters of Charity. He leads an active ministry from Little Portion Hermitage and Monastery in Arkansas and St. Clare Monastery in Texas. He is also a Grammy- and Dove-award-winning, multiplatinum-selling Contemporary Christian Music pioneer, and a bestselling author of more than thirty books.

https://johnmichaeltalbot.com
https://littleportion.org

———

Steve Rabey is a veteran author and journalist who has published more than fifty books and two thousand articles about religion, spirituality, and culture. He was an instructor at Fuller and Denver seminaries and the US Air Force Academy. He and his wife, Lois, live in Colorado.

steve@steverabey.com